Breathing Freely

Also by Ruth McGinnis

Living the Good Life: Simple Principles for Strength, Balance, and Inner Beauty

Praise for *Breathing Freely*

I finished the last page of *Breathing Freely* sitting in the doorway of an old barn, enjoying the midmorning breeze. The baby was asleep on a blanket. The sky was brilliant blue and the clouds were plump and white and glorious.

I cried for the beauty of it all . . . for the beauty of the words I had just read, for the reminder that life is beautiful and terrible and everything in between all at once.

For the first time in a long time I felt inspired to wrap my arms around the entirety of my own life—the people and the places that I cherish and cling to and am grateful for every day, and also the sadness that pulls on me as surely as the moon pulls the tide . . . for the bridges that I've burned and the faces that I miss and the feelings of loss that leave me quiet and still.

I breathed deeply, closed my eyes, and thanked God for the richness of it all.

Amy Grant, SINGER/SONGWRITER

Ruth McGinnis has captured the spirit of America and the home in her new book. You cannot love others until you learn to love yourself. A great read that I could not put down.

Donna Hilley, PRESIDENT AND CEO,
SONY/ATV MUSIC PUBLISHING, NASHVILLE

The difference in value between an inviting story and an inspirational myth is the difference between a changed life or merely a changed perspective. Ruth McGinnis invites each of us into the redemptive story of grace as she chronicles her journey to freedom with refreshing vulnerability and disarming honesty. To read this collection of personal vignettes is to be called into a larger narrative of restorative love. Ruth writes as she lives and performs, with healing sensitivity and the rhythms of eternity.

Scotty Smith, PASTOR, CHRIST COMMUNITY CHURCH, FRANKLIN, TENN.
AUTHOR OF *OBJECTS OF HIS AFFECTION*
COAUTHOR OF *SPEECHLESS* WITH STEVEN CURTIS CHAPMAN AND
UNVEILED HOPE WITH MICHAEL CARD

ACCLAIM FOR *LIVING THE GOOD LIFE*

How can I put into words the impact of the journey I began with Ruth? We started at the beginning . . . with balance, posture, and simple exercises—and we talked. . . . The simple exercises that Ruth and I have been doing for years, the exercise of respect toward myself and others, and the exercise of taking a simpler approach to life, have strengthened not only my body but my mind and spirit as well.

AMY GRANT, SINGER/SONGWRITER

In this delightful documentation of many of her life experiences, Ruth McGinnis has achieved her goal of writing a book that reflects simplicity, common sense, resonating with a quest for health more than a search for the perfect body.

KENNETH COOPER, M.D., M.P.H., BEST-SELLING AUTHOR OF *FAITH-BASED FITNESS*

In our work together Ruth encouraged me to exercise for the way it would make me feel rather than how it would make me look. The good life is about changing your life and becoming the person you always believed you could be, but were too overwhelmed to seek. A book for your soul as well as your body.

KATHY MATTEA, COUNTRY MUSIC RECORDING ARTIST

Reading [Ruth's book] is like having your own trainer and counselor to walk with you every day.

DR. PAUL MEIER, CO-FOUNDER AND MEDICAL DIRECTOR OF NEW LIFE CLINICS; COAUTHOR OF THE BEST-SELLING BOOKS *LOVE IS A CHOICE* AND *LOVE HUNGER*

In a book as warm and reassuring as a country doctor on a house call, Ruth McGinnis has not only given us a practical guide to healthy living, but shown us that getting—and keeping—fit doesn't have to take a lot of time or cost a lot of money. This is exactly what America needs to hear.

SENATOR BILL FRIST (R-TENNESSEE), M.D.

Ruth McGinnis makes a compelling case not just for a healthier lifestyle but for a life with meaning. Her approach to wellness is spiritually uplifting and leaves the reader with a sense of hope.

DR. ROBERT SCHULLER, PASTOR OF THE NATIONALLY BROADCAST THE HOUR OF POWER AND THE CRYSTAL CATHEDRAL

Ruth McGinnis's *Living the Good Life* is a wonderful book that offers sound advice on achieving inner and outer beauty without using trendy diets, fad fitness, or empty self-help theories. Her approach gives us hope that we can achieve peace and balance in our hectic schedules. Stop and smell the roses with Ruth, and learn how to enjoy the very good life our Creator has given us.

SHELLEY BREEN, MUSICAL RECORDING ARTIST WITH POINT OF GRACE

I spend more time overworking and handling "have tos," . . . so when I picked up *Living the Good Life*, I thought, *Is this* really *possible?* As I read Ruth's book I realized she's right: I don't have to be stressed out! God created me to enjoy life—even in my busyness. I popped Ruth's companion CD, *Songs for the Good Life*, into my player (she's also a professional musician), grabbed a glass of water, and enjoyed the melodic sounds of her violin. Now that's living *la vida buena!*

GINGER KOLBABA IN TODAY'S CHRISTIAN WOMAN MAGAZINE

Ruth McGinnis maintains that for people to be healthy they must become well-rounded individuals, incorporating diet, exercise, and rest into the health equation. She even deals with such lifestyle issues as the intrusion of television and its time-robbing effect upon our lives. Thoughtfully written, this book is a pleasure to read . . . the simple principles are universally applicable.

CHRISTIAN RETAILING MAGAZINE

With so many health-conscious books on the shelves these days it's refreshing to find one that really stands out from the crowd. Ruth

McGinnis . . . offers a sensible approach to living a full, healthy life, taking things one step further by exploring the spiritual and emotional balances. This book is perfect for anyone seeking an all-encompassing, healthy lifestyle, and who enjoys a great read.

NASHVILLE PARENT MAGAZINE

Breathing Freely

Celebrating the Imperfect Life

RUTH McGINNIS

Fleming H. Revell

A Division of Baker Book House Co
Grand Rapids, Michigan 49516

Published by Fleming H. Revell
a division of Baker Book House Company
P.O. Box 6287, Grand Rapids, MI 49516-6287

Second printing, December 2002

Printed in the United States of America

Library of Congress Cataloging-in-Publication Data

McGinnis, Ruth.
    Breathing freely : celebrating the imperfect life / Ruth McGinnis.
      p.   cm.
    ISBN 0-8007-5783-1 (pbk.)
    1. McGinnis, Ruth. 2. Christian biography—United States. I. Title.
    BR1725.M3125 A3 2002
    973.92'092—dc21   2002007524

For current information about all releases from Baker Book House, visit our web site:
http://www.bakerbooks.com

For John

Contents

Foreword

Weeks before receiving the manuscript of this book, I had been haunted by the words of theologian Paul Tillich: "We live lives that are hopelessly broken, *and we know it.*" No one is exempt from the intuition or flat-out recognition of our desperate human plight.

Some people become aware earlier than others. Some awaken through a midlife crisis, some through debilitating illness or addiction, some in the dark woods of depression, despair, and overwhelming fear. Others, caught up in the love of pleasure, trapped by fierce pride, or consumed by ravenous greed, are suddenly startled by a flash of insight that their lives are a senseless, chaotic blur of energies and their minds are a zoo from which most of the animals have escaped. Yet others are simply defeated through the painful discovery that efforts to extricate themselves from the shambles of their lives are self-contradictory, because the source of the shambles is the imperious ego. Thrashing about trying to fix themselves is an exercise in futility.

When the hopelessness of the human predicament is finally acknowledged and accepted, the inward journey properly begins.

The great spiritual masters and mystics affirm the truth of the ancient Eastern adage: "When the student is ready, the teacher appears." For many readers of *Breathing Freely*, Ruth McGinnis will be that teacher. In this lyrically beautiful memoir, she shares with uncommon candor her gut-wrenching trauma as a sixteen-year-old, the emptiness of pursuing a career in music as a classical violinist, the hollowness of human approval and adulation, and two tragic premature deaths, inducing a breakdown of her old world that led to a breakthrough into a new possibility.

"I started to look at life differently, less as a journey through peaks and valleys and more as a series of layers—layers of horrible and beautiful constantly weaving together like threads in a tapestry. To love life means learning to embrace this tapestry, this unspeakably complex backdrop against which the human drama plays daily."

I cannot recall a book that so movingly describes the decisive generational impact of parents, grandparents, and great-grandparents on the life of a young woman. After visiting the cemetery of a paternal grandmother she had never met, Ruth writes: "My grandmother's short life has left an indelible imprint on my earthly journey, a reminder of the mysterious human connectedness we all share. Her story has inspired me to feel and express every emotion along life's path. Her painful leaving makes a poignant case for the magnificent release of grieving. Her grave reminds me to seek beauty in the heartrending process of living but not to miss any part of it, especially the exquisite agony of the dying time."

Masterfully written, *Breathing Freely* offers a buoyant response to Nobel prize-winning poet Seamus Heaney's probing question, "How perilous is it to choose not to love the life we're shown?"

I recommend this book without reservation to anyone seeking to live gracefully in an imperfect world.

BRENNAN MANNING
NEW ORLEANS, LOUISIANA

Prologue
Summer 2000

Opening our arms to a day is an act of faith.
DAN ALLENDER, *THE HEALING PATH*

I SAT IN THE DARKNESS of the movie theater after seeing the film *Sunshine,** tears streaking my face. The credits rolled, and people around me started filing out, but I was frozen, stunned into recognition of the terrible beauty of this saga, a beauty I'd been seeking in my own life for a long time.

Since my early thirties I have been on a journey of self-discovery, a process of untangling the snarled strands of my sometimes unmanageable life, the quintessential quest of a Baby Boomer trying to find meaning in a cynical time. Along the healing path I have found emotional resolution, returned to my childhood faith, and charted a new course in my creative career, more in keeping with my true, God-designed gifts. And yet I have often felt more overtaken by the disappointment and losses in life than enthralled with its joy and possibility.

I identified with Ivan, I suppose, who speaks in the film's final narrative of the human desire for an enduring enjoyment of life. The only surviving descendant of three generations, Ivan is desperate to find meaning in the midst of the great modern age that wiped out his Hungarian-Jewish family,

Sunshine is a Hungarian film, released in the United States in 2000 by Paramount Classics.

the Sonnenscheins, who suffered years of fascist rule, the Holocaust, and Stalin's Communist regime. Ivan muses on what's mattered in life and sorts through the belongings of his beloved grandmother, Valerie, who has just died from heart failure in old age. As he studies pictures from the piles of beautiful photographs she'd taken since the turn of the century, her remarkable life emerges. Ivan remembers how she'd always urged him to find joy in life and how he'd always struggled through layers of existential cynicism to simply endure it. He remembers the words of encouragement she'd spoken to him shortly before she died: "Politics has made a mess of our lives. . . . still I've enjoyed waking up every morning. I've tried to take pictures of what is beautiful in life, but it hasn't been easy." His grandmother had sustained many losses—her husband to illness, her sons and all but one grandson to the Holocaust—and was forced to live her final years in one small room of the family home. And yet, with her resilient spirit, she chose to delight in the music she played on the piano and the taste of coffee with cream.

Try to photograph what is beautiful in life. As Valerie's words resonate with Ivan's own desire to live, he realizes that of the three generations of Sonnenscheins preceding him only she had known the gift of breathing freely in life.

The gift of breathing freely. The clarity of this idea—to breathe freely—was as startling to me as the lights coming up after three hours in a darkened theater. I thought of all the mornings I'd awakened without a sense of enjoyment for the day at hand; the long desert times when I was waiting for the right circumstances to line up so I could begin to live; the lonely years I'd spent away from my faith in futile attempts to carve a meaningful life for myself without the shelter of God, the years I'd lived by the credo, "My will be done." I thought of the beauty I'd not photographed because I was too busy taking pictures of things that didn't exist, snapshots of perfection, preconceived images of soon-to-be-forgotten achievements. I thought of all my years of frantic questing, trying to become someone other than myself.

The weight of it seemed unbearable—a weight of many layers of protection that I'd accumulated along my life journey—layers that made my shoulders droop toward my heart and my whole chest feel so heavy it was difficult to breathe.

I took a deep breath and then another and another, letting them out in a huge sigh.

Suddenly I began to understand a moment that had startled me years earlier in my thirties—why, when I returned to the neighborhood of my childhood, I sat on the curb across from the house where I grew up and cried. I'd seen the ghosts of my past—the children I'd played with and myself as a child and how I'd been blissfully engaged in a moment at hand, not invested in any outcome. It was a snapshot of life before I'd assumed the agenda of being perfect or learned the grown-up lessons of shame and fear and not-enough-ness. It was a moment of living life like the gift that it was, created for me. I cried then, like I was crying in the theater now, grieving a resilience of spirit I'd once enjoyed but that now often eluded me.

21

I thought, *All I ever really wanted is to breathe freely in the gift of life*.

Later I began to look for those free-breathing moments. I wanted to recognize and seize them in the present. But first I would need to retrieve them from my past. I realized I needed to sift through memory like Ivan with his grandmother's beautiful photographs. By doing so, I reclaimed the free beauty I had experienced when galloping on horseback across the plains of Montana with the wind whipping the hair across my face or when playing my fiddle under the stars on the banks of the Ohio River with my mentor and friend John Hartford— unfettered by the demands of classical perfection, stage fright, and my own ego needs. Most surprisingly I found beauty in the flawed moments, when the horrible darkness, such a contrast with loveliness, made the lovely moments clear—lovely moments I might have otherwise missed. The contrasts struck me: The agony of losing my favorite aunt, eased by holding her hand as she passed and sensing the ethereal release of her spirit in a golden haze; the painful bewilderment over career failures, illuminated by the creative integrity that could manifest itself in no other way; the heartbreak of loving unwisely and too well, tempered by the richness of it all and an enhanced capacity to feel.

In the ordinary landscape of every day, a remarkable picture began to emerge and along with it a reminder of the resilient spirit that I longed to recapture. This is how I found the way back to myself, how I embraced and learned to celebrate the imperfect journey of life.

one

Nashville Calling

Learning to Be Real

Two roads diverged in a wood, and I—
I took the one less traveled by,
And that has made all the difference.

ROBERT FROST, *THE ROAD NOT TAKEN*

YOU CAN DRIVE FOREVER and still not distance yourself from the considerable baggage of your life—the expectations of others or a strangling self-imposed perfectionism. How surprising then when people appear on your horizon at just the right time, like an oasis, offering refreshment or practical help. How unexpected when they nudge you, wittingly or not, toward deep healing.

IN THE LATE WINTER of 1986, nearly five years after graduating from Juilliard with a master's degree in violin performance, I packed all my earthly possessions into a Ford pickup truck and drove 900 miles from Upper Westchester County, New York, to Nashville, Tennessee, to pursue a wild dream. My journey had all the trappings of the proverbial artist's quest, hitting the road in search of fame and fortune with a guitar on my back and a song in my pocket . . . except I didn't write songs, and the instrument slung over my shoulder was a fiddle.

It was the bravest, craziest, and most essential of all my life's choices, leaving behind, as permanently as anyone can leave anything behind, the last vestiges of my long and careful preparation for a career in classical music.

After Juilliard I'd been floundering for a way to earn a living with music. I yearned to do something I truly loved but was torn between staying in New York City, where I'd lived for three years, and returning to the Los Angeles area. In L.A. I had many friends and even an old boyfriend with dependable contacts in the freelance music business, but I was still searching for something I'd never find in the safe predictability of my old California life. I just hadn't found it in the New York music scene either.

The hard, grown-up life lessons I'd managed to avoid in the cloistered environment of conservatory practice rooms were beginning to hit pretty hard. During the first three months of my post-graduate experience, my violin was stolen from the first-floor apartment where I'd lived for more than a year. This is every musician's nightmare, and for me it seemed like losing an appendage. The insurance company provided a loaner violin, but without the instrument I'd spent so much time with and knew to the touch, I began to lose musical confidence and identity.

It didn't help that I was really struggling financially. I was trying to make it on my own after having been supported by my parents for many years, and I possessed zero understanding of what it really took to survive. While I tried to drum up enthusiasm for taking orchestra auditions and teaching violin lessons, it became increasingly clear that my heart wasn't in it. There were so few attractive choices for making a living by playing violin that I felt paralyzed.

In the process of freelancing around New York, I stumbled on a new musical interest. The club scene was inundated at the time with the music made popular by the movie *The Urban Cowboy*, including Charlie Daniels's big hit, "The Devil Went Down to Georgia." I went out with friends one night and for the first time witnessed a real fiddler in action with a country band.

I was completely riveted. The fiddler played a bright blue electric violin with complete abandon, sometimes in tune and other times not, in places smooth and then scratchy. The crowd was going wild. I thought, *That looks like fun*, and then almost immediately, *I want to do that*.

The very next day I went to a used-record store on Broadway that I'd walked by countless times on my way to Juilliard. This time I stopped to rifle through old vinyl recordings of country fiddlers. I picked out a couple with names of people I'd never heard, but tunes I'd recognized from the night before, standard fiddle numbers like "Cotton-Eyed Joe," "Cripple Creek," and "Orange Blossom Special." I sat down with those records in my apartment, transcribing the music I heard into a form I could read—finally putting to use some of the skills I'd learned in dreaded ear-training classes. Then I started to play. With the careful dedication of a classical musician, I memorized a handful of tunes in tightly controlled classical style.

Before long I was sitting in with country bands at clubs around the Tri-State area.

I was, in truth, an awful fiddler. I sounded just like an uptight, classical player, who couldn't improvise her way out of a paper bag, playing a bunch of notes committed to memory. Still, pathetic as I was in terms of musical depth, I made a splash on the flourishing country music scene as a tall, long-legged gal who could "play the fire" out of the fast-moving popular fiddle standard "Orange Blossom Special." My technical skills earned the respect of other musicians, even as I struggled mightily with the millions of things I couldn't grasp in this new genre.

Thank goodness I knew enough to start taking fiddle lessons from a wonderfully versatile musician named Marty Laster. Marty, who lived on the Lower East Side, had made the transition from classical violin to every eclectic, free style of fiddling imaginable; he turned out to be the perfect teacher to help me. He made compilation tapes to introduce me to the enormous scope of this world—cuts by bluegrass legends Lester Flatt and Earl Scruggs and Jim and Jesse McReynolds, Texas fiddling greats Johnny Gimble and Benny Thomason, the brilliant, manic fiddler Scotty Stoneman, and the shining star of Nashville fiddling, Mark O'Connor. I wore out these tapes with constant playing and rewinding to play again, while my recordings by Itzhak Perlman and Jascha Heifetz gathered dust.

My parents, and others in my family, were horrified with this new musical direction. I couldn't blame them. They had paid for countless violin lessons, music camps, sheet music, strings, and rehairing of bows, in addition to making substantial investments in fine instruments and a Juilliard education. Re-creating myself at this point in life appeared to them as fatal a decision as I could ever make.

I struggled with what my parents were thinking and feeling and with my own feelings over the loss of the identity I'd borne since the age of eight. To assuage my guilt, I'd periodically drag myself to a real violin lesson and schedule a recital or two. I even continued to practice my classical literature for another two years. But the horse was out of the proverbial barn. I loved this new music, the backwards approach to bowing and phras-ing, and putting emphasis on the "and" of the beat. I wasn't making much money at it and my savings continued to dwin-dle at an alarming rate, but I couldn't resist the wilder, freer road of country music.

A PHONE CALL in the fall of 1983 would bring an end to my awkward straddling of these two disparate worlds and set my internal compass firmly in the direction of the road to Nash-ville. A woman named Sherry, who fronted a band called Stonewall Junction, had heard my name at one of the many jamborees I'd played. She needed a fiddler for a special event coming up—her band was opening for a Tanya Tucker con-cert in Rockland County, and the fiddle player she usually called for special events wasn't available. Would I be inter-ested in taking his place?

Looking back, I consider it a small miracle that I didn't pass on this opportunity. Though thrilled that my name was in circulation, I still didn't feel like a real fiddler. I was terribly insecure about my abilities to perform—not just sitting in with material I knew I could ace but really performing with a band, playing backup lines and fills and solos on tunes I surely wouldn't know.

I took so long to respond to her simple question, she must have thought the line had gone dead. Finally, I asked as nonchalantly as possible, "Could you send me a tape of the numbers you'll be performing for the show?"

She talked me through the numbers planned and promised to send me a tape. In the meantime, I wondered what I had agreed to do. I hadn't recognized even half of what she'd rattled off, standard material that any self-respecting fiddle player would know—songs by Emmy Lou Harris, Hank Williams Sr., Kenny Rogers, and Tammy Wynette.

Without those practice tracks, I knew I'd be helpless. As soon as they arrived, I scheduled a lesson with Marty, and we set to work.

I showed up at the Tanya Tucker concert, nervous as a cat but well prepared. I had a brand-new, shiny black electric fiddle, just purchased from Manny's in New York City, and a borrowed amplifier, along with cords to plug in with and a little gadget called an equalizer, preset at the store to help enhance my tone. I even dressed for the night—tight black jeans, black cowboy boots, a new country-western shirt with a V-shaped yoke and ruffles. Most important, I'd carefully worked out and memorized every supporting part I would need to get through that gig.

As unrehearsed as we were, the set we played went well, and I fell into easy camaraderie with the eclectic group of musicians that made up Sherry's band. Our grand finale, which featured me on "Orange Blossom Special," was a predictably smashing success. I basked in the warmth of their compliments and those of the audience members who came up to rave over our group's performance.

Then I watched from the side of the stage as Tanya Tucker put on her show, my first up-close glimpse of a real country star in action. Intrigued with her fabulous clothes and kittenish stage presence, my fertile imagination ran wild. Naively, I thought, *She must have a really great life.* I dreamed about what it would be like for me to have the stage, the lights, and the applause of the audience.

Sherry called me again one week later. Would I be interested in playing one of Stonewall Junction's regular venues, a small club called the Golden Spur in Ossining, New York? The Golden Spur gig wasn't as well paid nor nearly as prestigious as the Tanya Tucker event, Sherry said, but if I were willing to do it, the whole band would love it.

As she spoke, I felt a familiar reticence descend on me like a wet blanket. All my life as a performer I had needed to be perfectly prepared. I knew I'd done a good job at our first engagement, but I'd never played a whole night of music with a country band. Fortunately, I decided to make myself vulnerable and admit my fear of not living up to expectations, at least not based on what I'd pulled off at the Tanya Tucker concert.

Sherry's response proved to be one of those moments in life that you look back on and realize how your destiny shifted on the weight of a few words. "Come play with us anyway," she said. "You know enough tunes to get through the night. You can turn your volume down on the stuff you don't know and just play along when you want."

The welcome relief Sherry provided in the midst of what was a truly difficult time—freely offered, with no expectations attached—cannot be adequately described. The best I can do is this: In my fledgling attempts as a fiddle player, I'd started to build a tiny bridge across a vast canyon that separated me from my innate, creative gifting. Then, out of nowhere, this marvelous human being called to me from the other side and threw a rope ladder all the way across. All I had to do was reach out and grab onto it, which was, by far, one of the bravest things I've ever done. After all, there is no greater trial by fire for a perfectionist than being exposed as a mere mortal.

That first night with Stonewall Junction I could not have been more human. It was a nightmare, really. I frantically bowed open strings, trying to follow chord changes I couldn't yet hear, and only sheer determination kept me on stage through that evening and in many to follow.

But what a gift! After living with the unforgiving scrutiny of classical music for so long, Sherry had given me permission to be flawed, unprepared, and imperfect for months on end. She never winced at a sour note and never once cast a dark look in my direction. A healing space started to open inside me. It would take many years for this healing space to grow large enough to balance out the relentless perfectionism I've applied to every area of my life. But in the safety of a mentor—my friend Sherry—I had the freedom night after night to play it all wrong, get paid for having fun, and take the chance to do it better the next time.

IN A MUSIC CIRCUIT that stretched from Long Island and Greenwich Village to Putnam County, then Connecticut, New Jersey, and all points in between, our band had crossed paths with many musicians and different styles of country, folk, and bluegrass music. Sherry and I, especially, enjoyed our gigs farther north in an area of New York State that nestles up against the Catskill Mountains. We shared an attraction to the music and dancing emanating from there, rooted in bluegrass and oldtimey styles. And so we decided to treat ourselves to a week of jamming with those musicians and learning traditional dances like the Contredanse and Texas Two-Step.

In the summer of 1985, we left for the Fiddle and Dance Camp in Ashokan, New York. For Sherry, who had decided to go back to school and finish her degree in biology, the camp was kind of a last hurrah. For me, it was a long-awaited chance to see for myself visiting artist Mark O'Connor, by far the hottest fiddle player gracing Nashville's music scene at the time.

Neither of us expected this week to prove itself to be a pivotal event in our lives, but, from the first moment, we sensed the magic of the place. The camp was saturated with the world of acoustic music, complete with rustic accommodations, a constant pickin' of tunes around picnic tables and campfires, and dances every night in an outdoor pavilion on top of a wooded hill. We sat at the feet of legendary Tiny Moore, mandolin player for years with Bob Wills and the Texas Playboys, as he regaled us with tales of life on the road, including how the band touched up their shirts with white shoe polish between infrequent launderings. I marveled at the virtuosity of Mark O'Connor, whose playing in person was every bit as astonishing as what I'd heard on records.

For the camp's closing events, Jay Ungar, camp founder and versatile composer and instrumentalist, had created a breathtaking tradition to mark the end of his Fiddle and Dance weeks. After the last dinner and camp talent show, he stood up in front of the group with his fiddle and started playing "Ashokan Farewell," a haunting Celtic-flavored melody he'd written a few years earlier but only recently recorded. You might know the tune as the prevalent theme throughout Ken Burns's documentary *The Civil War* for PBS. I will forever associate it with Fiddle and Dance Camp—and a new vision for my musical career.

As Jay started the second strain of this bittersweet tune, other instruments joined in, filling in the beautiful harmonies. Then Jay turned, walked out the door of the dining hall where we'd gathered, and led us like the Pied Piper through wooded paths lit only by the stars. We wound around to the pavilion on the hill for the final dance, but it's that walk through the woods, the strings of our acoustic instruments resonating, that lingers in memory. Surrendered to a moment when time seemed to stop in the world, we were fearless in the dark, connected to each other only by a thread of melody—as free as the breeze rustling through the trees.

I left Ashokan more determined than ever to surround myself with influences and opportunities I needed to flourish as a fiddle player. I started making plans to move to the city where country music artists make dreams come true.

BARELY SIX MONTHS LATER, on a bleak February day, I hit the road to Nashville, my truck packed to overflowing. I was towing an equally packed U-Haul trailer, which I'd discovered too late wouldn't accommodate the box spring to my double bed. But nothing was going to slow me down from following my dream.

I started south—right into a snowstorm in Pennsylvania. Gripping the steering wheel for dear life, I expected to slide off Interstate 81 into a ditch at any moment. By the time I reached Woodstock, Virginia, I was exhausted. I checked into a cheap hotel for the night and slept fitfully, adrenaline still pumping through my bloodstream.

The next morning the beauty of the Shenandoah Valley surprised me. The storm clouds had parted, leaving behind wisps of fog that hung around the mountains like Christmas tree garlands. The sun shone brightly on an unlikely combination of early spring green grass and patches of snow. I continued my journey south as though in a dream, marveling at the beauty and singing along with Emmy Lou Harris's "Leaving Louisiana in the Broad Daylight."

By the time I reached the Tennessee line, I was into The Eagles and crossed over the border of my new home state with "Hotel California" blaring from the stereo and me sobbing. Driving alone in my truck for many hours, away from my friends and fans on the East Coast, far from the glow of my success in small-time music venues, I could no longer avoid the serious questions that haunted me: *How will I make a living here? How can I possibly compete with the caliber of these musicians? What if I can't make it in music?*

The enormity of the choice I'd made was hitting me. A person could take only so many detours in life, and I would probably never do anything so wonderfully reckless again. I was on the brink of a brand-new life at age twenty-nine, as exhilarated as I'd ever felt, and scared to death.

AS I PULLED INTO NASHVILLE, the sun was setting in the west. My new, temporary lodging was in the home of a friend of a friend in the Madison area, east of town. It was a basement apartment that had been rented to wandering musicians many times. In a couple of days I settled into my room and then jumped headfirst into every musical or social opportunity I could find.

Within weeks I was working on a fairly regular basis as a musician in one way or another. The work wasn't what I'd dreamed. In fact, during that first year, I found myself doing what I had said I would never do again—playing in a string section for various studio recording dates. Many musicians deemed this attractive work, but I'd done enough high-stress, fiercely competitive studio sessions in Los Angeles to know that I loathed it.

However, something always comes from something just as surely as nothing comes from nothing. Something came soon in the form of many new friends in the Nashville recording scene. One of these musicians called to see if I could replace him on a gig at the last minute. "Ruth," he exclaimed, "I have a great opportunity for you, playing with John Hartford."

I didn't answer immediately, musing whether or not this would be a worthwhile gig.

"You know who he is, don't you? He wrote the Glen Campbell hit 'Gentle on My Mind' in the late sixties. He was a regular on *The Glen Campbell Show* and on *The Smothers Brothers Comedy Hour*. He is an artist in his own right, a real legend. This is a perfect gig for you. You've got to take it."

I'm embarrassed now that the dots had to be connected for me regarding the legendary John Hartford, the man who would influence my creative career more than any person before or since. Also it seems odd to describe John as legendary and then feel compelled to explain why, but that was the essence of his character. His rich talent was part of the artistic bedrock of Nashville, but so many people—me included—never knew who John Hartford was until frequenting his world or getting a rare, honest glimpse beneath the often superficial layers of the mainstream country music business.

His "Gentle on My Mind" stands as one of the most recorded and broadcast songs of all time, but John Hartford was never impressed by the business of music. He preferred to play bluegrass, write songs from the heart, and indulge his passion for riverboats. After a stunning commercial success that would have seduced most musicians to keep clawing up the show biz ladder, he'd left behind the glitz of L.A. to return quietly to the music that first beckoned his heart—the traditional, old-time bluegrass he'd heard growing up in St. Louis.

He was a musician's musician, now focused on writing and recording music that featured three-part fiddle harmonies—and I happened to be in the right place at the right time to fill in for the fiddle player who had to drop out. As my acquaintance said, the opportunity was tailor-made for my unique abilities. I could play like a fiddler *and* read music. But there was plenty to learn. With less than thirty-six hours before the first gig, I practiced and memorized chart after chart of intricate harmony lines.

As the last weekend of May melted into June, I made my way to the Summer Lights concert in downtown Nashville. I'll never forget my first sight of John Hartford, whom I'd never seen but whose music had already captured my imagination. He was off to the side of the outdoor stage with the other players in his band, getting ready to rehearse for our performance, which was later that afternoon. Slim and tall—about my height of six feet—he wore a white shirt, black vest, and black Derby hat that would have seemed outlandish on anyone but him. He had a beautiful, sculpted face, jutting cheek and jawbones, a straight aristocratic nose, and deep-set eyes that twinkled above a pixie grin. He was holding a banjo strapped across his shoulder, ever ready to pick a tune, and that is exactly what we proceeded to do.

After the briefest of introductions, he launched into "The Ohio River Rag," the trickiest of the songs I'd prepared on short notice. With a performance so close at hand, I'm sure he was anxious to gauge the abilities of this new-to-town fiddler and last-minute sub. I too was anxious—wanting to prove what I knew I could do and dazzle this man and the rest of the band with my musical skills and careful preparation. As John counted off "The Ohio River Rag," I felt the exhilaration of perfect musical belonging and joined in confidently, as though I'd been part of his group for years.

We finished running the tune, and John looked at me with a combination of relief and something akin to awe. Then he gave me his trademark bow, hands pressed flat together, fingertips just below his chin, dipping toward me from the waist.

I'd passed muster, delivered the day. I was officially a member of the Hartford String Band.

I PERFORMED WITH JOHN'S string band off and on for about three years. I say off and on because Hartford was primarily a solo act, traveling the country in his bus, usually with only a bass player—the one-of-a-kind Roy Huskey Jr.—in tow, as many as two hundred and fifty days a year. But between that 1986 Summer Lights performance and the eventual dissolving of the string band, as John moved on to new musical frontiers—and he always was moving toward some new passion— I logged unforgettable time and experience with him.

I loved our session work in 1988, working on a string band album, the second and perhaps my favorite of all his recordings—*Down on the River*. Until the happy day I started making my own records, ten years later, this project provided months of the most enjoyable session work I'd ever done.

In 1987 and 1988 John took the string band to Colorado with him for the Telluride Bluegrass Festival and on a flurry of road trips to nearby states, usually Illinois, Kentucky, and Ohio. In Nashville we played at the annual Fan Fair, a memorable concert with the Nashville Symphony at Riverfront Park, a Fourth of July Bluegrass show at Opryland, and we made multiple appearances at the venerable Station Inn, where the best bluegrass musicians in the world have performed for decades. Tucked behind a modest exterior on 12ᵗʰ Avenue South, this rustic, family oriented, strictly bluegrass club is a revered Nashville treasure.

Throughout this nearly three-year period, I remained under the spell of Hartford's magic, drawn in by the integrity and passion he had for everything he did, which was much more than just being a musician. In fact, from our first meeting, I was about as smitten with John Hartford as an aspiring artist could be with a beloved mentor. My heart beat a little faster in his presence, my imagination was seized by the diverse expressions of his many passions, and I was spellbound by his stories, experiences, music, and every word that came out of his mouth.

Every time I watched his unique genius, I realized I'd stumbled on something life changing. This quirky, irreverent man would weave magic with an audience. He played his banjo and fiddle, sing-talked his way through wonderful story-songs, and intermittently accompanied his music with the patter of his own feet against a sand-sprinkled, amplified slab of plywood. Unaffected by the stage and spotlight, and with effortless grace, he was simply so completely himself that it almost hurt to watch.

His musical and creative authenticity was the perfect antidote to the contrived, formulaic approach of churning out artists in the industry I'd moved here to join—not that John Hartford's influence prevented me from chasing down any number of misguided ambitions over the years, but his artistic purity pricked the conscience of my own authentic yearnings as I struggled to find my musical identity.

For years my downfall as a creative person had been defining myself through my projects, rather than the other way round. I had more creativity bursting through me than I could contain, and I harnessed it again and again to unrealistic goals that I thought would make me look good but had nothing to do with my truest gifting. For example, shortly after arriving in Nashville, I'd determined to add singing to my artistic agenda in the hope of landing a record deal. I'd sung backup for Sherry fairly competently in the Stonewall Junction Band, and my voice wasn't terrible, but it wasn't solo quality either. Of course, this didn't stop me from making myself miserable by adding yet another thing—voice lessons—to the long list of frustrating pursuits.

Eventually I managed to attract the attention of a well-meaning, aspiring producer. We put together a high-quality demo tape, but since I hadn't the slightest idea what I really wanted to do, I fell back on predictable, trite material suited for the flashy fiddle players who were in vogue at the time.

After months of hard work in the studio, I played the three-song demo for John, hoping desperately that he'd like what I'd done. He listened intently to each song, then responded in his typically honest manner. "You are so much better than the material you're playing," he said, adding something I've never forgotten, though the truth of it would take years to sink in: "Don't make the mistake of becoming famous doing something that's not you, because whatever makes you famous is what everyone around you will keep making you do to stay famous."

John had some experience with this. After his huge success with "Gentle on My Mind," he was encouraged by many people to write another "Gentle on My Mind." He later said he had done it—by writing spoof lyrics to fit perfectly over the same melody. So his advice to me was what he told aspiring artists throughout his life: "You have to do what's in your heart. If you do, and people like it, that's great. But even if people don't like it, then at least you haven't wasted your time doing something that's not you."

It was easy to take such advice because I saw John living what he believed. It's well-known that when he was growing up in St. Louis, he'd been mesmerized by the majestic riverboats that drifted down the Mississippi. He said to me once, near the end of his life, "I wanted to be the complete river man." Though he ultimately pursued the music he loved to Nashville and Los Angeles and back to Nashville again, he didn't give up his passion for the river. He found a way to weave his love of the river into his music, his songs, and his life. He lived in a wonderful Victorian-style house on the outskirts of town, overlooking the Cumberland River, so he could watch the boats pass; he did, in fact, learn the ways of a "complete river man," earning a pilot's license and for many years captaining the *Julia Belle Swain* out of St. Louis for several weeks each summer.

What fascinated me was the way his diverse passions breathed life in and out of each other. Having grown up with a compartmentalized, tightly structured approach to everything I did, the Renaissance quality he brought to his creative life was like a breath of fresh air. He was a riverboat captain and virtuoso player of the banjo, fiddle, mandolin, and guitar. He wrote songs and books and mastered the art of calligraphy, which appeared on many of his published works and album covers. He was a historian of old-time fiddle music and the fiddlers who created it. He could make his whole body into an instrument for music, from the shuffle of his dancing feet against a sandy piece of plywood to the wonderful washing machine sounds he could make with his mouth. None of these interests interfered with another; the fact that he expressed himself so completely in everything he did only added to his integrity as an artist.

I never got the feeling that John did anything creatively he didn't want to do or that wasn't a natural extension of his heart. His considerable performer's ego was grounded in the confidence that the adulation he received from his fans was not for any facade he'd erected for that purpose; when he performed, he was generous, sharing his art as he longed to experience it. He never forgot that the audience was the most important part of the show.

I will always be grateful that John embraced me as a kindred spirit. Whenever I was in his presence, I sensed a shared affinity for those serendipitous moments in life, so full of poetry you almost have to rub your eyes and look again to believe what you are seeing. The truth of this occurred to me one summer evening in 1989 as John and I and the rest of the string band sat on the deck behind the Executive Inn in Owensboro, Kentucky. We were warming up for a performance for the International Bluegrass Music Association Awards Show, and sitting on that deck gave us the feeling of being in one of John's favorite places—right on top of the water.

It was a hot, cloudless summer night, and a gentle breeze came off the river, which shimmered beneath a full moon's glow. We rambled from one string band selection to the next, the sounds of our instruments wafting out and disappearing over the water. Eventually we were playing perhaps the loveliest of all Hartford's songs, "The *Delta Queen* Waltz." John sang the lyrics, which he had written in honor of one of the riverboats he so adored:

> *Oh the whistle came out, such a deep mellow sound in the
>   night*
> *And the echo came back from a shoreline of twinkling light,*
> *There was nothing we really could say,*
> *The River had swept us away,*
> *Like a present hereafter, the warm sound of laughter,*
> *As we danced to the* Delta Queen *Waltz.*

Sensing a movement on the horizon, John and I looked upstream at the exact moment, just in time to see the *Delta Queen* ease around the river's bend, heading straight toward us. We locked eyes in amazement at this little glimpse of heaven—a gift of beauty and grace—that had just appeared out of nowhere. I had a feeling that I've only experienced a handful of times in my life, when nature, sound, and the pure sensation of being completely inside of a moment washed over me. I knew John was awash in the moment too. It was like a lingering dream—the moon, the river, John's lyrics to that song, and of all the riverboats to traverse that stretch of the Ohio that very night—the *Delta Queen*.

This cherished memory and all my memories of John remind me there are no accidents in life. I was destined to fall in love with his pioneering spirit as surely as I was destined to begin a career in alternative forms of music years earlier with my wonderful friend Sherry. I needed these individuals to come into my life like I needed oxygen to breathe; surely they are testaments to how God's hand plants people, like grace, in our way and clears a path forward.

Along the long road that brought me to Nashville, I can see God's fingerprints all over my life. If I had not met and had the wonderfully encouraging and musically healing experience of working with Sherry, I doubt I would have found the desire and courage to move to Nashville. And if I had not moved to Nashville, I would not have stumbled into the rare opportunity to work with John Hartford.

His gentle admonishment from so many years ago to not make the mistake of defining myself doing something I didn't love spoke deeply to my heart and soul. It has brought me back to the drawing board more times than I can count over the course of my career, as I have struggled to connect with the flawed beauty of my innate, God-given creativity. John showed me that you have to do what you know how to do and be yourself in your art or else on some level you die.

While I'd struggled to make sense of my own diverse interests, all along I had hoped to one day be as completely myself as John was himself, to be as transparent and real as I watched him be. I loved breathing the air that he breathed partly because I wanted to absorb his creative purity into my bloodstream. I could never be like John because I am me, and that was just his point and what God used in the example of John—to make me see that being oneself is more than enough, and the only dreams worth striving for are your own.

Two

The Road to Decatur

Journey Back

Only the most mature of us are able to be childlike. And to be able to be childlike involves memory; we must never forget any part of ourselves. If we lose any part of ourselves, we are thereby diminished. If I cannot be thirteen and sixty-one simultaneously, part of me has been taken away.

MADELEINE L'ENGLE, WALKING ON WATER

IT'S EXACTLY 365 MILES from where I live in Nashville, Tennessee, to my hometown of Decatur, Illinois, a six-hour drive under the best of conditions—beautiful weather, no traffic, few speed traps, one pit stop.

I joke that I've worn a groove into the road to Decatur with my many trips there. I started these regular pilgrimages in 1986, after moving to Nashville, the closest I'd lived to this place I love since I was twelve. The easy driving distance to my hometown, and its proximity to my favorite aunt, lured me back—that and the fact I felt closer to myself in Decatur than I had since leaving home eighteen years earlier.

At first I didn't fully realize why I needed to go. I just went—back to a place I remembered as happier, easier, where I could just breathe. The road spoke to me, and the simple landscape of my childhood beckoned as though it set the magnetic true north of my internal compass.

Now I understand the attraction. I needed to recover the parts of me that I'd abandoned along life's way. If I'm ever to make sense of my restless, gypsy life, it's by reconnecting with the confident, carefree eight-year-old I once was, the girl who knew what it was like to feel comfortable inside her own skin.

So I set out on this road that's become geographically familiar but emotionally full of new adventure. I take one of my dogs, my beloved Akita, Jojo, as a traveling companion, and I take my time—to decompress from whatever busyness has enveloped me—to reflect.

AFTER AN HOUR on the road, when I cross the state line into Kentucky, the journey north feels like a firm commitment. There the scenery shifts as if by magic. Long green fields signal horse country, and ancient gray barns and shimmering lakes dot the countryside. This landscape continues uninterrupted until the outskirts of Paducah, where I usually plan a rest stop before crossing the Ohio River into the state of Illinois.

The first time I made this drive I crossed over that mighty river and burst into tears. The sign THE PEOPLE OF ILLINOIS WELCOME YOU did me in, drawing forth long-buried, pleasant memories of growing up in the Land of Lincoln.

I loved the comfortable two-story brick house we moved to on West Riverview Street in Decatur. At five I enjoyed the privilege of having my own small room, one of the perks of being the oldest of (then) three girls. I'll never forget Mrs. Gustin, next door, welcoming us with a fantastic cake shaped and decorated like a house, an indication of the easy friendliness we would enjoy with our neighbors for years to come.

Our street was lined with well cared for houses, varying in size and design, one yard running into the next, separated by flowers and shrubs and only an occasional fence. The whole block felt like one big playground to me. I was as comfortable spending time in the charming playhouse behind the Gustins' house or "playing fort" under the huge pine tree three doors down as I was in my own backyard.

My parents were young and enjoying especially good years in their marriage. With only two younger sisters, it was easy for me to get lots of attention from my mother. Apart from her Thursday night choir rehearsal and Sunday morning church service, where she juggled the jobs of organist and choir director, she was a traditional, stay-at-home mom. She cooked, sewed, cleaned, and ironed constantly. Sometimes, after making a dress for herself, she would sew one for me out of leftover material, and I knew no greater thrill than showing up at church in a dress matching my mother's.

She read to us every night before bedtime and helped us with the alphabet and vocabulary skills, giving us a head start in school. She also taught us how to play the piano, with weekly lessons starting for each of us around the age of five.

I felt like the queen of the family in this uncomplicated world. As the oldest, I was her big girl and little helper, and I loved getting to do everything first. When I picked up the violin for lessons at the age of eight, it felt so special to have this instrument all to myself. The musical competition and sibling rivalry that my sisters and I would later develop was hidden somewhere beyond the horizon.

Dennis School, where I completed kindergarten through fifth grade, was a pleasant six-block walk away. My mother accompanied me just a few times to help me learn the route. It was as normal then as it is unimaginable now for a child to walk that distance with only the company of other children or even alone.

I loved going to school, especially every fall. The freshly sharpened pencils, clean notebooks, and brand-new textbooks always seemed to announce the start of a new adventure. One of my favorite things was a huge tree near the playground that dropped beautiful, fresh buckeyes, a coveted prize if you could find one before the other children picked them up.

My little group of friends gave me comfort here, and I always felt safe in the hallways and on the playground. My self-confidence was strong enough to withstand even the high dork factor of carrying a violin to school on orchestra day, which I started to do in third grade.

I wasn't without fear in those days, but my greatest anxiety was that I might get sick at school and join the ranks of the unfortunate kids who threw up in class, usually all over a desk. There was one poor boy who managed to do this every year. But as much as I dreaded this humiliation, I never had to endure it.

During summer I walked to school for an arts and crafts program that took place around picnic tables on the west, shady side of the schoolyard. There, in the humid breeze of hot summer days, I learned with other kids how to weave boondoggle and make plaster of paris figurines, which we would later paint. My favorite molds were the shapes of animal heads—horses and dogs—a clue to passions I'd explore later in life.

NOW, AS I TRAVEL, I look over at Jojo, who clumsily turns around, trying to find a more comfortable spot, then settles back down, interrupting my thoughts. I'm on the long, bleak, sleepy stretch of old concrete highway, through a part of southern Illinois that offers nothing more to my view than walls of rock and scrubby foliage.

Farther north, the closer I get to Decatur, the beautiful farmlands start to appear, especially when I leave the interstate at the Salem-Sandoval exit and head west to Highway 51. On this two-lane highway, my favorite stretch—and part of the Lincoln Heritage Trail—there's nothing but farmland as far as the eye can see. Occasionally, quaint small towns appear, tiny places that don't seem to change much from year to year.

First there's Vernon, with the funky antique/junk stores at the foot of town, then Shobonier on the way to Vandalia, Illinois's original capital (until 1839), filled with Lincoln historic sites. Farther ahead, past a state penitentiary, on the right side of the road, is an old silver-gray barn that looks like something out of an Andrew Wyeth painting. I've wanted to take a picture of this barn—perched on a hill, dignified despite its dilapidation—for years. But with my destination close now, I'm reluctant to stop. I'm getting closer to that place where I once breathed so freely.

MY DECATUR DAYS INCLUDED the fairy-tale elements of a unique friendship, a devoted aunt, and an intriguing neighbor next door. The same year I started playing the violin, a new family moved in across the street. Wes Tilley, who taught at Millikin University where my father was a professor of music, and his wife, Barbara, became great friends with my parents, often coming over for after-dinner drinks or dessert and rousing games of paddle tennis on the Ping-Pong table we had in our basement. Their shy, attractive, seventeen-year-old son was my first secret crush; more important, their twelve-year-old daughter, Virginia, became my first best friend.

Virginia Tilley was by far the most sophisticated kid I'd ever met. I was always in awe of her, and flattered that she would spend so much time with a scrubby little eight-year-old kid. I was mesmerized by her imagination and varied interests, which included a model horse collection, C. S. Lewis's *Chronicles of Narnia*, and later, acting out scenes based on a new television show, *Star Trek*.

We spent hours exploring the nooks and crannies of the fabulous tree-lined alley that ran behind my house, even parking ourselves by a neighbor's cherry tomato plant one summer day, salt shaker in hand, to feast on the plump fruit.

Another layer of magic was added to my life when my strikingly beautiful aunt Cathy moved to Decatur from Albuquerque, New Mexico, where she worked as a nurse. My dad's youngest sister was, quite simply, the perfect aunt. She was a grown-up, but younger, more modern and dashing than any of the other adults I knew. She wore her hair in sleek pony-tails or French twists, used bright-colored lipstick and powder blue eye shadow, had a terrific sense of style, and looked like a movie star when she lit up a cigarette and crossed her long legs. My aunt gave by far the best birthday and Christmas presents and was my favorite person to accompany to the movies, especially Julie Andrews's musicals, which were very popular at the time.

Aunt Cathy provided the additional drama of dating and eventually marrying the bachelor farmer who lived next door. Marshall England had moved into the neighborhood a few years earlier, a gentleman farmer with 2,300 acres of prime Illinois farmland just outside of Decatur in the small town of Warrensburg. When Marshall moved in, my mother welcomed him to the neighborhood with the Midwest tradition of a freshly baked cake. I thought he was a grand addition to the street. Elegantly handsome, this interesting bachelor would come home from long days working his farm to pour himself a drink, grill a steak, and then spend several hours working in his beautifully landscaped backyard.

My mother invited Marshall over to have dinner with us from time to time, and I'm sure this is how he and my aunt first met. He was a charming dinner guest and seemed genuinely interested in me and my sisters. One Easter he surprised us (and my meticulous mom) with a basketful of ducklings he'd found on his farm. My sisters and I enjoyed the rare treat of having pets, albeit in a pen outside, until they got too big for our back-yard and had to go back to the country.

When my aunt started dating Marshall, who was sixteen years her senior, our next-door neighbor became even more fascinating. Cathy would join him for drinks and steaks, and they would visit for hours in his screened-in back porch or work together in the yard. Marshall's lifestyle, home, and personality were replete with every ingredient to enthrall my youthful imagination.

This fairy-tale chapter of childhood ended the same month that Robert Kennedy was assassinated. As the nation was reeling in sadness over the loss of yet another of its leaders, our family made the wrenching move away from everything that felt safe and familiar to me. My father, disillusioned with his job at Millikin University, had taken a promising position at what was then San Fernando Valley State College, in the Los Angeles suburb of Northridge. Driving away from the house on West Riverview, waving good-bye to my best friend and favorite aunt, I sensed, as only a twelve-year-old verging on adolescence can know, that the halcyon days of my youth were over.

AFTER THE GENTLE PACE of Decatur, the sprawling suburbs outside of Los Angeles felt like a different planet. The self-confidence I enjoyed in the safe confines of Dennis School evaporated after changing schools twice in six months' time (as our move from a rented house to our permanent home included a change of school districts), twice bearing the onus of "new kid in class." Carrying my violin to school on orchestra rehearsal days cemented me in the role of nerd. Before leaving Decatur, I'd mastered a pretty good kick in the game of kickball, even impressing the boys in my class. But this impressed no one on the hip playgrounds of Southern California. Here marching in formation from playground to class (which I'd never done), handball (which hurt my hands), and a unique torture—swinging from rings (impossible with my long arms and legs)—were the order of the day.

In addition to excelling in nothing considered cool, I'd begun an awkward growth spurt that would continue through high school. While other girls were sprouting admirable curves, I was just getting taller and more gangly. My pant legs always seemed too short, despite the decorative trim my mother kept adding to the hemlines.

By the time I started seventh grade, and yet another new school, I was firmly established in the ugly duckling phase of adolescence. Cementing my low self-image were the braces on my teeth, unfashionably flat shoes that I wore to diminish my towering stature, and my uncontrollably frizzy hair (exacerbated by a thick layer of fog that rolled into the San Fernando Valley most mornings).

I'd stare with envy at the popular, pretty girls with their straight, glossy hair, long eyelashes, and perfect white teeth. These were the girls who had developed early and well—their busts, waists, and hips proportioned beautifully to an average height of five feet, five inches. I wondered what it would feel like to be like them, to strip and shower fearlessly after gym class, excel in dance or gymnastics or cheerleading, have cool clothes and even cooler boyfriends. I was doing well to avoid running into the surly group of guys who gathered around a cluster of lockers not far from mine and found great sport in calling me Tiny Tim.

I began to develop a rich fantasy life, imagining what it would be like to be pretty, accomplished, and accepted. To feed this life, I became almost neurotic with a need for solitude. But in our bustling household, which had grown from three children to five, and even with my own room, there was no way to escape the constant sound of music being practiced. Two of us now played the violin, one played the cello, and all of us played (and were expected to practice daily) the piano. With my talented, competitive sisters coming up behind me, I felt the pressure to retain the family crown.

The violin, once an instrument of magic and pride, had become the focus of my identity and self-worth, a symbol of how well I was doing in life and my rank in the family. Coupled with the common teenage feelings of never being enough was a grandiose plan of what my future life would be. I projected images of such epic proportions onto the blank screen of my unfolding life, there wasn't room for anything flawed and real.

My expectations of myself became relentless. Life began to feel hard.

THERE'S A NEW LOOP of interstate that circles Decatur now, which could speed me to the final destination of my aunt's house in Warrensburg. Instead of taking the loop, though, I always pick up Highway 48. That highway runs right by my old neighborhood on West Riverview, past Millikin University, where my father taught music for seven years, and past Fairview Park, the site of countless picnics, Sunday afternoon drives, ice-skating in the old open-air pavilion, and walks around the duck pond with bread in our hands.

I continue along the same road my mother used to take east through town, toward the Congregational church where she worked as the organist and choir director. Instead of turning right on Pershing Road as she used to, though, I turn left, toward the small farming community of Warrensburg where my aunt lived most of her married life.

As soon as I enter Warrensburg, I can barely contain the feelings of anticipation flooding through me. I can almost smell dinner cooking on the stove, see my aunt Cathy's warm welcome, hear the sound of her voice, and feel her enveloping hug. That's the way it used to be, but my aunt is gone now, stricken with lymphoma during her sixtieth year. My Uncle Marshall is an old man, bent from years of farming, bent and pained by the storms of eighty-three years, especially the loss of his beautiful Cathy.

As I make the final, tight turn between the stone pillars on either side of the gates, now propped open to receive me,

I think about how this place and this uncle by marriage have become so important to the life I celebrate. We have been through good and hard times together, just like the seasons that I always loved here in Decatur.

I've missed the Decatur seasons. When we moved away from here, my soul yearned for the changes in season that California could not provide. The biting cold and darker skies of Decatur winters only made the holiday season with its warm comfort food, bright Christmas decorations, and fires in the fireplace seem more festive.

In California I'd tried to find comfort in milder changes, but our first Christmas was a depressingly sunny, eighty-two-degree day, not conducive to sipping hot chocolate by the fire; before that, the hot, dry Santa Anna winds made me miss even more Decatur's crisp autumn with the changing colors of the leaves. In Midwestern days, I'd raked those leaves into soft mounds that I could jump into; then my father would burn the piles at the curb as I watched. It was sweet, that smell, sweet like belonging—which is what started me on this journey and what I'd been searching for all along.

The belonging I'd felt in Decatur was never completely taken from me. It was just buried. The sense of safety imprinted during those formative years was still there, just blurred by time and circumstance.

I take a deep breath and step from the car. How good it feels to be back.

Three

Detour

Secret Places

I have come to believe that by and large the human family all has the same secrets, which are both very telling and very important to tell. They are telling in the sense that they tell what is perhaps the central paradox of our condition—what we hunger for perhaps more than anything else is to be known in our full humanness, and yet that is often just what we also fear more than anything else.

FREDERICK BUECHNER, *TELLING SECRETS*

WHEN I LOOK BACK on the summer of 1973, I'm resolute in my belief that you must be able to claim the events of your life in order to know and celebrate who you are. For many years, however, the memories of this defining, adventurous time were the most carefully concealed secret of my life. I feared what others might think if they knew all that had happened. How could I see that there is something more painful than making known the secret parts of the self?

IN AUGUST 1972 I was fifteen, and graduation from junior high school two months earlier had marked the beginning of a new chapter in my life, coinciding with, among other things, the happy event of getting the braces removed from my teeth. Though far from being one of the popular, pretty girls my age, I sensed light at the end of the tunnel for my ugly duckling phase.

For the first time the prospect of going to a new school didn't seem threatening either. Leaving Patrick Henry Junior High was a relief in many ways. No longer would I have to confront a hallway frequented by the boys who called me Tiny Tim, or the sobering, empty locker that was once used by a friend who had tragically died during the ninth grade.

Granada Hills High School held the promise of a unique creative outlet I secretly pined for too: Highland dancing. My imagination was completely captured by a select troupe of twelve girls who, clad in full Celtic regalia, including kilts imported from Scotland, performed traditional Scottish dances at the football and basketball games. The coveted position of Highland dancer, second only to cheerleader in prestige, wasn't achieved through looks or popularity but through specific ability to master the classic Scottish dances like the Fling and the Sword Dance. Layered, as I was, with insecurities, the prospect of becoming a Highland dancer gave me hope. Dance of all kinds had long been one of my natural interests and abilities, and I intended to work all year toward my dream, preparing for the auditions which were held at the end of the school year.

In the meantime, another unique opportunity was developing. For some time I'd been the regular baby-sitter for a family in our neighborhood. They were taking a family vacation to Montana, a three-week adventure that would start and end at a western ranch and would include travel throughout the state, plus stops in both Yellowstone and Glacier National Parks. Since the father of the family would join them only near the end of the trip, this mother asked me to go along to help with the children. Having another adult in the picture would make her vacation much more enjoyable.

Her recognition of me as an adult, and the descriptive, adventurous travel plan overcame whatever initial reservations I had about taking care of three energetic kids for several weeks. In fact I was thrilled. I'd spend time on their relatives' cattle ranch, get away from music lessons for a while, and break free of my family for a summer.

My parents agreed—as long as I took my violin and had time alone to practice each day. The plan was put in motion.

My mom took a picture of me at the airport on the day of my departure, surrounded by my dad and four sisters. It reminds me of what a momentous occasion it was for each of us in my family. Big sister Ruth was leaving home for nearly a month, taking off for parts unknown.

FROM THE MOMENT THE PLANE touched down in Montana, I felt my inner landscape make a continental shift. I was mesmerized, intoxicated, and completely seduced by this beautiful place. The expanse and depth of the sky, the rugged terrain, the dryness of the air, and a Wild West flavor permeated everything and spoke to my soul like no place I'd ever been. Something I'd sensed for a long time began to strengthen as a conviction—I was a country girl at heart. This revelation would prove to be one of the truest things I've come to know and celebrate about myself.

Away from the supervision of my parents for the first time in my life, I made another interesting discovery. Left to my own devices, I was content to leave my violin sitting in the closet untouched. I guiltily enjoyed this new freedom from daily practice. As time went by, however, I also ached for the protection of my family. The truth was I'd taken on a job more difficult than I could have imagined.

The children, who behaved reasonably well for me in their own home, now became unruly to the point of making my life miserable. In addition, their grandparents, our primary hosts while in Montana, seemed to dislike me. The grandmother, especially, missed no opportunity to point out my many defects. I didn't wash fruit, like a banana or an orange, before peeling it and giving it to the children. I offered them too many choices and therefore couldn't control them. My peanut butter sandwiches, instead of bologna and cheese, were not nutritious. When I scrubbed the Teflon-coated frying pan too vigorously one morning after making breakfast, I scratched the surface and this sealed my fate. I became the scapegoat for everyone's frustrations.

I found myself in a truly dumbfounding situation. I sensed whenever I walked into a room where my employer was talking with her parents that they were saying disparaging things about me. Nothing in my upbringing had prepared me for handling such dynamics.

In retrospect I see that, at fifteen, just out of junior high, I was too young for the scope of responsibilities this job entailed. My skills as a sitter were fine for two- or three-hour stretches from which I could then escape. However, navigating the minefields of being a sort of guest-employee in someone else's home—someone with whom I had no history or relationship—was a different matter altogether.

In the midst of this strained environment, I found relief in the company of my employer's relatives, who owned the beautiful ranch we often visited. I'd never experienced a truly out-in-the-sticks taste of rustic life, and from the first of our many visits there I felt myself swept up with renewed enthusiasm for the splendor of Montana. I remember waiting for the owner, a man in his early forties whose ruggedly attractive picture graced the guest room I occupied at the grandparents' house, to join us at the end of his long workday. I already felt more at home on his ranch with his wife and two children, a boy and girl just a few years my junior, than I had since leaving California. Plus I looked forward to my first glimpse of a real cowboy-rancher.

As he drove up the long dirt road leading to the farmhouse, and the profile of his cowboy hat and chiseled jaw became more defined, I had the sudden impression that I was seeing a knight in shining armor. He seemed to be the perfect cowboy archetype, the rugged man of the West. When he pulled up beside the house where we waited, he tipped his hat to me, and I felt as though I'd met my rescuer.

That evening, as the kids and I prepared to go horseback riding, he carefully assisted me in saddling and getting on my horse. He commented on my natural ability to sit the animal and praised my handling of the children in front of the others in a way that made me feel vindicated as a baby-sitter. At every opportunity, he included me in the ranch activities planned for the kids' vacation; he complimented me in ways I'd never been praised before. When we roped and wrestled a calf to the ground, he described me as being "strong for a city girl."

His attention became a balm to my self-esteem. He acknowledged a budding prettiness in me every time his eyes met mine. Indeed, I'd changed a great deal in the previous few months. The ugly, metal braces no longer adorned my teeth, and long awaited curves finally arrived on my beanpole frame. But I still believed I was an ugly duckling.

Starved for some kind of acceptance, and desperate to mentally escape my challenging baby-sitting job, I carried the new sensation of being noticed and admired by a grown man like a shield against the criticisms that continued to be aimed in my direction. The kids seemed to delight in making me miserable, and their mother continued to treat me with cool politeness, so I fantasized about the cowboy who had entered my life. Our return visits to the ranch and his company, sandwiched between road trips to Yellowstone and Glacier National Park and visits with other relatives scattered across the state, gave me the strength to hang on for those three weeks. When he took me in his arms one evening, out of sight of the others, to seal his affection for me with a secret kiss, my fantasy of rescue was complete.

It never occurred to me that the attention of this married man was inappropriate or misguided. The heady feelings of what I believed to be a harmless romance were mixed up with the overpowering emotions I was experiencing, a sort of soul connection, to the wild and beautiful Montana.

I loved every inch of the state, from the rugged ranchlands outside Billings to the sprawling plains of the Indian reservations near Helena and on to the dramatic splendor of the national parks. The freeness of the ranch lifestyle was weaving a spell over me. I ached to leave the constraints of my life in California and move here, planted forever in some rustic farmhouse at the end of a long winding road, with my own horse, some chickens, and a cow.

This romanticized view, of course, was part of my adolescent understanding. In light of my secret crush on the cowboy-rancher, I was curiously comfortable with his family, bonding easily with his wife and children. My teenage fantasy was a separate entity, not connected to the reality of his family or the fact that I liked them all very much. So when the topic of hired help came up at the dinner table, on one of our last evenings at the ranch, I was envisioning my Montana dream coming true. Every summer, during their busiest season, this ranch family hired a local girl to help with putting up hay, rounding up cattle, and other day-to-day chores. The next summer's job description included relocating to a new, larger, and even more beautiful ranch on the flat top of a mountain; the ranch family liked me so well, they wanted to pay my airfare, in addition to wages, to bring me back as the hired help.

My employer, whose attitude toward me seemed to warm considerably on the flight back to Los Angeles, greeted my parents with this news and rave reviews of the trip. I'd really hit it off as a ranch girl, she said, and her relatives were so impressed they wanted to fly me back as an employee the following summer.

I'm sure my parents would never have agreed to the plan had it not been for the illusion that the ranch family were somehow our friends. After all, they were related to our friendly neighbors. So, through several letters, the details were worked out for my three-month job.

The following June, I was once again on a plane headed north. The continuation of this grand adventure broke the mold of anything I'd ever done. Surely I was going to test the limits of my strength in managing animals, children, and the land. I had not thought much about the cowboy-rancher since I had left Montana and never imagined that the challenge of a physical relationship lay ahead of me as well. I simply hadn't connected the dots—and perhaps was too naive to do so— between the flirtation that had begun the previous summer and the sadly predictable outcome. Neatly filed away in my memory was the safety I'd felt because of this man's attention and protectiveness. All I could remember was the joy of being put on a pedestal and praised at every turn.

I arrived in Montana for the second time a few weeks shy of my sixteenth birthday.

MY NEW EMPLOYER, the cowboy-rancher, met me at the airport—alone. He'd come straight from a long day in the fields and reeked of body odor. The image I'd held of him from the previous year was undergoing rapid adjustments. Suddenly he seemed rougher, older, more flawed; his presence, which once gave me security, now made me uneasy, even repelled me. Something wasn't right. I was too young to completely understand the situation, but I sensed that what had been for me an innocent infatuation was not so innocent for him.

As we drove toward the ranch, the implications of his attentions the previous summer became clear. He told me how much he loved, adored, and physically longed for me. He leaned toward me, pleading his cause, as I froze in my seat of the old, black Ford pickup truck. Dumbstruck, I stared out the side window, feeling this was somehow my fault and sensing I was in over my head. I told him haltingly I'd come back to the ranch because I loved it. I simply wanted to work there.

He told me he expected physical intimacy.

I began sucking in huge breaths of fresh air from the open window to dilute the overwhelming smell of him. There seemed to be no answers. *What to say? What to do?* My mind scrambled for options. *When we get back to the ranch, I'll tell his wife what's going on, and enlist her protection. . . . No, I can't possibly tell her anything. I'll call my parents and tell them I've changed my mind about spending the summer in Montana. . . . But how can I tell my parents, with whom I've never even talked about sex, about the mess I've created?*

I loved Montana and wanted to be there. I began to think that somehow I could manage this cowboy, that I could negotiate a compromise.

These combating thoughts flooded through me, none of them helpful, until we arrived at the ranch, where the family greeted me enthusiastically. I concealed my discomfort the best I could and gave myself over to the joy of seeing the kids again and returning to the beloved ranch. My pursuer backed off and, in the context of his family, seemed the secure rescuer-provider I'd remembered. He was even likeable.

By evening, while out on a horseback ride with the children, I'd relaxed and once again felt the seductive pull of Montana on my soul. I was still considering my options, but leaving just didn't seem to be one. I told myself it would be okay. I was a grown-up. Feeling invincible on the wide Montana range, I consigned myself to the unfolding drama.

SEARED INTO MY MEMORY is the long-kept secret of that summer and the vivid details of five sexual encounters with a man old enough to be my father. At the time, I told myself that crossing the threshold of womanhood at the age of sixteen was no big deal, that it hadn't been violent, and that on some level it was consensual. But the reality was that this crossing was the result of a series of strongly coerced relations with my married employer. Beneath that adolescent bravado was unbearable shame.

For three months I did a bizarre dance of love and hate, attraction and revulsion, control and manipulation with the cowboy-rancher. My susceptibility to his attentiveness, charm, and overtures of intimacy only increased my confusion and shame, for despite my genuine reluctance to be physically involved, I struggled with the natural hormonal drive and sexual curiosity of a teenager and with my initial attraction from the previous summer. I was struggling too with my protected, well-churched upbringing, which had always taught me to associate sex with the institution of marriage. I knew what I was doing was wrong. But I was away from my home and church, and all the rules seemed to be changing. The truth was that I was engulfed in murky waters I didn't know how to navigate.

It was a survival mechanism to keep thinking of this man as my rescuer. He was the one who bought me a horse that would be mine alone, a brown and white, mule-tailed Appaloosa gelding I named Comanche. He was the man who showered me with gifts disguised as essential cowgirl gear—jeans, shirts, cowboy boots, and the hat I'd need for long rides on the range, rounding up cattle.

From thirty years' distance, I can see that the sense I had of being elevated to a pedestal and worshiped was no illusion. His flattering attention met my deep need to feel all grown up. Whatever sickness lay at the root of this man's twisted agenda, he continued to express a genuine interest in who I was, what I liked, and my opinions on everything from buying horses to the politics of the Vietnam War. Most compellingly, he shared and encouraged my love of the land and life on the ranch. My fascination with the rough beauty of Montana was met at every turn with what seemed to be his genuine desire to help me drink deeply of my experience there.

It was confusing. For all my adolescent naïveté and misconception of how God intended a man and woman to love one another, I'd truly grown and matured in other areas while on the ranch. I was living with the greatest sense of freedom I'd ever known, breaking the mold of my careful upbringing, and finding within myself diverse longings and abilities I didn't know I had. I traded the skill I knew best—playing the violin, which once again languished in its case—for other strengths I clearly possessed but had never developed.

Within a few weeks I'd become an accomplished horseback rider, sitting the saddle as well as any cowboy, even capable of riding bareback. My arms and legs had newly defined muscles from constant riding, lifting heavy logs in the process of building fences, shoveling muck out of trampled watering holes, and toting bales of hay, heavy blocks of salt, and huge bags of grain. I'd proved myself a valuable asset in putting up hay, learning to the surprise of everyone (including myself) to operate with ease a tractor and hay-forklift. I also dealt straightforwardly with the raw, earthy realities of life on a ranch, from the branding, ear-tagging, and castrating of calves to trapping and then disposing of dead porcupines.

Every day I overcame another level of city-girl squeamishness and fear. I loved my newfound sensibilities. I could milk a cow, saddle and bridle a horse almost without thinking, drive a pickup truck (though still months away from getting my license), and exercise the uncanny gift of "cow sense"—knowing when a particular cow was preparing to bolt from the herd during roundups and intuitively urging my horse forward at just the right time to cut off a break before it happened.

These accomplishments were complemented by a natural, seamless connection I began to feel for the outdoors. I'd always loved the woods, beaches, mountains, and water, but I'd never been so permeated by the forces of nature as in Montana. I couldn't get enough of the vast horizon and sprawling landscape. Montana had the bluest sky, contrasted against gold-green grass—colors and textures so amazing I'd feel so physically full of the beauty of the earth that I could barely contain the pleasure of such loveliness. I'd stand on the mountaintop where the ranch was located, with my arms outstretched to feel the full impact of a strong wind, or, after a long day of stacking bales, I'd climb up to the top of the haystack, so I could watch the sun set.

The force of such feelings—for a land and a lifestyle—were mixed with the powerful emotions I was dealing with in my first physical relationship. This struck me one night as I sat with the rancher and his children on the edge of a hill. We stilled ourselves to watch the fiercest thunderstorm I'd ever seen. As lightning split the sky and wind blew down a pelting rain, I had the brief sensation of being part of the storm, rather than just an observer, pulled into a vortex I couldn't control.

I felt this again during the final stretch of a long, grueling cattle drive near the end of my stay, when the heavens seemed to open and rain poured down. We galloped across the last, long, hilly field toward the corral, with cattle hoofs thundering and the horses almost flying, the storm deafening. Everything in that moment seemed connected to everything else. But like the merging sounds of clapping rain, thunderbolts, hoofbeats, and the pounding of my heart, my pure love for a beautiful land and a taste of freedom had merged with the

imprisoning victimization of a tainted relationship. I had yet
to learn how to distinguish between them.

I LEFT MONTANA at the end of the summer with mixed emotions and a sense of loss. I had, in fact, lost my innocence in
Montana, and in leaving ranch life on the range, I thought I
was also losing the first profound beauty and creative freedom
I'd ever known.

Before heading home, I lumped all these events together
as a single experience and told myself: I've become a woman.
I've learned to interact with a man and negotiate a relationship, and I've survived. But in my first private moment
I wrote a blistering letter to the cowboy-rancher, fully vent-
ing the true feelings I'd been too afraid to express while
under his authority. I told him I despised his aggression and
would never return to his clutches. Although I couldn't
name what had happened to me, my letter was an attempt
to recognize my sexual abuse and his calculated, predatory
behavior.

The San Fernando Valley I returned to was covered in
smoggy haze, and the houses seemed built one on top of the
other. I reentered my family unit, showing off new muscles
and the pictures of me chasing cows and buffalo on horseback, and I picked up the violin again for daily practice.
Once more I was on the well-rutted path of my musical
upbringing.

In high school I pursued my ambition of becoming a larger-than-life violinist, earned a Highland dancer position, and met my first real boyfriend (pretending and acting like I was still a virgin), and I kept my secrets secret.

As I tried to re-create myself, I developed an ability to rewrite my personal history in my own mind. This meant burying the summer of 1973 in memory, despite the nostalgic enchantment I felt for Montana every time I took Comanche (who later came home with me) for a ride. It took me years to figure out it was not the seduction of beautiful Montana but my other seduction that I wanted to seal off in some secret place of my heart.

NEARLY THIRTY YEARS after that summer of 1973, I'm still haunted by feelings of sadness and shame. The memories of sexual abuse are like broken shards from a mirror on my life. Worst is the reflection I see of a lovely young girl in a horribly devastating relationship. It has seemed too painful to behold, this sharp, disjointed fragment. But other reflections shine as perfect moments: the first sight of that magnificent ranch on the flat top of a mountain, the times I felt the wind blowing through my fingers and hair, the times I wrapped myself completely around a horse to gallop like one creature across an open field; best is a glimpse of great truth from that summer—the truth that the wild beauty I'd found wasn't just in Montana, the place, but inside myself. In all the confusion and difficulty, I'd discovered there a relentlessly creative, free spirit that simply would not fit the preconceived mold of a classical violinist, though I would spend many years trying to be one.

This is the lesson of owning our mistakes or failings, our disappointments and sufferings. Any honest look back on one's life will surely reveal something almost too painful to remember. More painful, though, is what we miss when we don't celebrate all that we see.

For so long, whenever I looked at my life, in the present or in memories of the past, I wanted to see only perfection. I feared anything less, so much that I learned to close off myself from anything that didn't fit into the well-planned life. I carefully arranged a facade to cover the exquisite vulnerability we share as human beings. For, though the events of our lives are as unique to us as our fingerprints, we will each receive inevitable, deep physical, sexual, emotional, and spiritual wounds; this is the common ground of our humanity.

It's in revisiting and reclaiming the imperfect, wounding, most painful events that we can celebrate our full humanness. Though painful to behold, what we see when we gaze beneath our careful facade doesn't kill us. It makes us real, whole, and free to be all we were created to be, despite the expectations of ourselves or a world so eager to define us.

Had I not chosen to own this secret part of my life that carries my greatest shame, I could never celebrate that sixteen-year-old cowgirl self when, for one scary but unforgettable summer, I discovered the truest longings of my heart that emboldened me years later to leave behind the expectations of myself and others on a journey that would reconnect me with the holy source of all my gifting.

four

Rough Roads

The Dying Time

The hurt of loss is too hard, then there is the incomprehensible fact that the loved person simply is erased from the planet. The basic facts of birth and death I've never remotely been able to fathom. . . . I can't take non-life.

FRANCES MAYES, BELLA TUSCANY

THERE ARE INFINITE WAYS to experience loss, or what I call "the dying time," and each time the pain of it feels too hard. Yet dying times hover constantly. Hold your hand in front of your face, maybe an inch away from your nose. That's how close death or loss is. You can try to avoid this awesome reality, tucking accidents, disappointments, and the bad news that comes from the other end of a phone line far away in the deepest recesses of consciousness. It's easier to distract yourself with work, social events, and material things or to be lulled into the pretense of a culture that celebrates youth and a certain kind of beauty as weapons against mortality.

But at some point the reality cannot be ignored or hidden, and it won't go away. Not everyone can die peacefully in sleep at the age of ninety-five after living a wonderful life. Those who do die peacefully, you can be sure, did not live without some disappointments and loss too.

The year I began to resign myself to the dying time, I saw how it might hone my appreciation for the rich tapestry of life. In fact I started to look at life differently, less as a journey through peaks and valleys and more as a series of layers—layers of horrible and beautiful constantly weaving together like threads in a tapestry. To love life means learning to embrace this tapestry, this unspeakably complex backdrop against which the human drama plays daily.

THE PHONE RINGS, and I make an awkward but much practiced maneuver to step over the dog gate from the kitchen where I'm making dinner. I dash to the other side of the house just in time to beat the answering machine.

It's my cousin Andrea calling from Boston, in tears. "Something terrible has happened," she says. "Belly was hit by a motorcycle today."

Belly was the tiny, blind beagle, rescued from euthanasia at birth by Andrea's mother, my aunt Cathy, and given to Andrea only six months before Cathy would lose her battle with lymphoma. Little Belly, who navigated quite well without eyesight, nose perpetually in the air, sniffing and sensing her way around, had accompanied Andrea through a rough stretch of transitions spanning five years. Belly had been there for Andrea's last months of college in Michigan, through a long summer spent in hospital room vigils at her mother's bedside, on to graduate school in Arizona to pursue a poetry degree, then back home in Warrensburg, Illinois, for her mother's death. Belly came with her to visit her elderly father and was with her for a few hopeful but difficult years in Boston. A loyal companion through loneliness and sadness, Belly had given my talented but floundering young cousin the most comforting relationship in life.

I listened and winced at the description of the accident, upset to the point of tears myself. "She was tied up outside the market where I was shopping. I came out and unhooked her leash only for a second. She ran out . . . and . . . she died instantly."

It was too easy for me to imagine the scene, being well acquainted with the finite margin for error that exists between the worlds of motor vehicles and furry creatures. I imagined the self-recriminations that probably had begun to run through Andrea's mind: *If only I had . . . I should have . . .* I ached for my cousin, knowing her grieving and regret had only begun, and the terrible scene of the accident and empty spaces Belly used to fill would haunt her. But how do you share what you know in these moments about the tapestry of life? How do you identify these horrible strands as dying times that can be embraced?

WHEN I WAS FOURTEEN, my best friend in California was killed while riding her bike after school. Theresa Molitor was an advanced-placement student with a brilliant life in front of her. Everyone expected this pretty brunette to go on to law or medical school. Our small group of close friends especially gravitated to Terry. Every day before first period English, my best confidante, Jackie, three guy friends, and I would gather near Terry's locker to visit.

So the Tuesday morning we showed up as usual and Terry wasn't there, we wondered why she was uncharacteristically late. A boy who lived on Terry's street saw us and delivered the news: Terry was dead, hit by a car the previous day while riding her bike in the afternoon. My friends and I scoffed at what we assumed was just a tasteless prank, but the seventh grader persisted in his story. Then the sober expression of our homeroom teacher, walking toward us, confirmed the sad news.

That day had a dizzy, spooked quality. Nothing seemed real. I sat in English class, staring at my best friend's empty desk, listening to our teacher tearfully talk about what an exceptional, bright student Terry had been. Our group huddled together during recess and lunch, filling in one another on what we'd heard about the events of the day before, simultaneously discussing Terry's funeral and expecting her to walk up to join us at any second.

After school, still in a daze, I walked in our house and told my mom what had happened. She was sitting in the den with mending on her lap, totally unprepared for the story of Terry's death. At the news, her face crumpled in anguish, and she made the wailing sound that only a mother can make, imagining, I'm sure, what it would be like if this had happened to one of her children.

I skipped dinner that night. I stood behind the house on our makeshift basketball court. Alone, I shot hoops in a trance, feeling as far away as I ever had from the love of God.

Terry had been confirmed as a member of the Catholic church in a joyful ceremony just weeks earlier. Now, unbelievably, the church was the site of a death visitation, a funeral, and a burial. My friends and I filed past Terry's open coffin for a last glimpse of her. It was the first time I'd ever come face-to-face with a dead body.

Terry was wearing her confirmation dress, beautiful as ever, but her eyes were closed and she seemed so still. Years later, this is still how I picture her—stiff, lying empty in that coffin.

We followed the funeral procession to the cemetery and watched as the casket was lowered into the ground.

"Ashes to ashes, dust to dust," the priest began.

Where was God? I wondered. *Where was God for Terry?* Thus began a long, spiritual estrangement as I declined to be confirmed in my own church a few weeks later, my fledgling faith crushed.

MY PATERNAL GRANDFATHER had died of cancer at seventy-four, my maternal grandmother of a heart attack at eighty-three, and my step-grandmother at eighty-one. But aside from natural deaths in our extended family, I didn't grapple with the larger issues of life and death again until my mid-thirties. Then the steady trickle of the dying time caught my attention.

The best friend of a guitar player I was dating, an anesthesiologist named Dunkin Nelson, dropped dead of a heart attack while out running one hot Sunday morning in July. He was just thirty-six. He and a friend were deep into the wooded trails of Warner Park when Dunkin suddenly pulled up short and said, "I have to stop for a minute," then collapsed to the ground, never regaining consciousness. His friend, also a doctor, started resuscitation efforts, screaming for help between rescue breathing, and was joined by another early morning runner, an athletic trainer who helped administer CPR. That trainer, John Burrell, whom I would eventually date and marry, told me later that he thought Dunkin had died almost instantly, that he'd turned blue and cold long before the ambulance and emergency rescue team arrived.

My boyfriend, like everyone who knew Dunkin, was left reeling. I too was shocked. The dying time, after all, impacts us most when it strikes someone we think to be too young, too beautiful, or larger-than-life to die, or when it claims the life of a person to whom we feel especially attached. But my own experience with the sudden death of my fourteen-year-old classmate had taught me the lesson very well: Death happens out of nowhere. A phone rings, the news is bad, and in fact is the very worst news.

So, still haunted by the shell I'd confronted of Terry Molitor, I decided against looking into the coffin of the once vibrant, happy-go-lucky Dunkin. I wanted to remember him the way I'd last seen him, full of life and enthusiasm during the intermission of a Pat Metheny concert.

After the service, friends and family returned to Dunkin's home for the food, drink, and milling about that follows the vacuum of death. As badly as I felt for Dunkin, his stunned widow, and my grieving boyfriend, I was moved most by the sight of Dunkin's golden Labrador, sitting in his pen, curious over the throngs of people, patiently waiting for his master to come home.

I began to think more about Dunkin's memorial service, held at a church he'd never attended, officiated by a pastor who had never met him. The combination of ideas—belonging, aloneness, future, past—kindled an awareness inside of me. *Maybe,* I began to muse, *investing in one's spiritual life is a good idea.*

A FEW YEARS LATER, in the winter of 1996, I made a fortuitously timed journey north to visit my Uncle Huby and Aunt Lois in Montana. Huby, my mother's only brother and her elder by eighteen years, was more like a grandfather to me. Now, after a series of strokes, he was languishing in a nursing home. I decided to fly from Nashville to Missoula, Montana, then rent a car for the drive to my aunt and uncle's home in Hamilton, in the cold of January. I brought my fiddle along to play for my uncle, who also had played violin as a boy, taught lessons during his college years, and never missed one of my recitals or school concerts while living near us in California.

Along the road to Hamilton, I thought of my unique attachment to my lumbering, gruffly affectionate uncle, and his wonderful wife, Aunt Lois. Our lives first became intertwined in the late sixties when shortly after my family made the move from Decatur to Southern California, Uncle Huby and Aunt Lois treated our whole family to a magical day at Disneyland. It was their generous way of welcoming us to California and making up for all the birthdays and Christmases not celebrated together when we'd lived so far apart.

With their own children grown and married, Uncle Huby and Aunt Lois took a keen interest in all of us girls, especially in our musical activities. They were always there to support us. They were also there to help my parents finance the fine instruments we needed when we headed off to college.

When Huby finished his long career with the Federal Aviation Administration, he and my aunt realized their dream of retiring to Lois's childhood home in the sleepy town of Hamilton, Montana. After years of sitting at a desk, Huby relished the beautiful outdoors in Big Sky country, the easy access to fly-fishing, and the quaint routines of small-town retirement. Living in the house where Lois had been born and attending the tiny Methodist church where they'd been married half a lifetime ago must have felt like the gentle closing of a beautiful circle.

I loved everything about their home in Hamilton. From the window of the upstairs guest bathroom, you could see the jagged skyline of the Bitterroot Mountains. The yard, though smack in the middle of town, sprawled across an acre of land and lent a rural feeling to the ninety-year-old house. A large garden was kept behind the house, where raspberry bushes grew that provided Aunt Lois with the fillings for her delicious, flaky-crusted pies. Inside the old shed beside the house, my uncle kept his "Hupmobile," a lovingly restored and maintained antique car from the 1920s, a latent passion that he indulged in retirement.

Whenever we visited, Uncle Huby and Aunt Lois focused on all our varied interests; Huby took us to his favorite fishing spots, equipped us with rods and wading boots, and taught us to fly-fish. My aunt called a cousin who had a ranch nearby to set up an afternoon of horseback riding for me, which was a particular passion at the time. On one memorable family outing, we picked quarts and quarts of huckleberries at a nearby farm, then returned to the house where my mom and Aunt Lois spent the rest of the day expertly canning, preserving, and making pies from the harvest. At the know-it-all age of seventeen, I watched this scene in the kitchen with respect, knowing I was witnessing a timeless, if waning, tradition.

When Huby and Lois celebrated their fiftieth wedding anniversary in 1988, my parents, sisters, and I, along with cousins, aunts, and uncles we hadn't seen in years, joined them for a luxurious weekend of great meals and family time at the beautiful Grouse Mountain Lodge in Kalispell, Montana. It was the quintessential family reunion, toasting Huby and Lois, reviving and creating memories.

Now, though, I was arriving in Montana to find Huby confined to a wheelchair and a nursing home bed, with reduced mobility and an inability to swallow.

I watched Aunt Lois fuss with Huby's socks and straighten his pillows and blankets, and I listened to her talk a usual and always-entertaining blue streak. Even though her once tall, handsome, and always genial husband could give little in return, it was profoundly important for her to visit Huby, anticipate his every need, and wrap her life around him. She had embraced the dying time, for—though I didn't say this at the time—it was clear Huby was ready to die. He seemed in a world of his own, even when alert and interacting with us.

The day I left, he was running a fever and had to be transported to a nearby hospital for observation. I knew in my heart this was a one-way trip. A special van arrived to pick him up, wheelchair and all, to move him to his new location. I clambered into the scary looking vehicle to finish my good-byes. I started to say, "Maybe in the spring, I could come visit again," but the calm look of acceptance on Uncle Huby's face stopped me short. We both knew we would never see one another again.

I struggled with what to say. Finally, I knelt beside him for one last hug. "I love you, Huby," I said. And "I know Jesus loves you." In the years since attending my friend Dunkin's generic funeral service, I'd made some awkward movement back to faith. Now my clumsy efforts to attend church and open my Bible once in a while were bearing fruit. The words sprang from some place inside me that had been wrestling with the concept of eternity and had finally given in.

My staunchly religious, Methodist uncle teared up and looked straight into my eyes with corresponding honesty. I never felt more connected to him than at that moment; it's what I think of when I remember him today.

Twelve days later, I received the news that Huby had died in the hospital. I packed and made travel arrangements to return for the funeral, thinking how it was both wonderful and strange to see my aunt twice in one month.

Back in Hamilton, Montana, I found Aunt Lois flattened. She must have known Huby's death was coming. Still, she seemed unprepared for the reality of losing her husband of fifty-eight years. She would let out long sighs that deflated her whole body.

The morning of the funeral, I sat with her at the foot of her bed, as she tried to pull herself together. She hadn't dressed yet and was still in her well-worn chenille bathrobe as she related the events of the night Huby died: "They called me from the hospital at about one in the morning. When I got there, Huby wasn't conscious. His breathing seemed shallow. I didn't know what to do except take his hand and talk. I talked about how the kids were doing and the grandchildren. I talked about our friends Roger and Olive, the weather, the local news. An hour later, he just stopped breathing."

She watched his face for a long time before leaving.

That weekend I witnessed that strange lingering that follows a dying time—the gathering of relatives, the reunion of family and friends. My parents made the trip from California, and my mom's sister, Crystalle, arrived from Oregon. Aunt Lois's house was full now with her two children and their spouses, so my folks and I stayed at a nearby hotel. How glad I was to have recently had Lois all to myself. Now I was more than content to mentally prepare for playing at Huby's service and to catch up with family members I'd not seen in some time.

Throughout the planning, the service, the church dinners, the after-funeral hangout in my aunt's living room, and all the activity surrounding this end-of-life ritual, I felt the gaping absence of my uncle's large, comforting presence. Huby's clothes hung in the closet with his scent lingering on them. His shaving lotion and hairbrush still sat on the bathroom counter opposite my aunt's toiletries, just as they had for years. The recliner in the living room, where Uncle Huby liked to sit and watch television, spending countless evenings with Lois, was empty. All of these things mutely testified that Huby once had been there but was there no longer. I thought: *This is how it will be for each one of us sitting here in this room. One day it will be my mother, my father, my cousin, and me that people will gather for, weep over, and decide what to do with a life's accumulation of material possessions.*

As I headed back that day to what seemed a busy, complicated life, I felt the strong urge to retreat from my responsibilities for a while, to rest and recuperate on every level. I longed for some space and time alone to let the events of the past month sink into me. Our culture rarely allows it. But embracing the dying time demands it. Dying times require that you see the importance of trusting that inner voice that directs you to visit a person *now* rather than later. How grateful I am for heeding that voice, for flying to Montana in the dead of winter with uncharacteristic spontaneity, armed with my fiddle, vivid memories, and a lifetime of affection.

I cherish the time I had with Huby, especially his last days. I couldn't change his circumstances, but I could play music for him. I could tell him how much he had meant to me over the years and the difference he had made in my life. I learned the lesson you can never learn too well, which is to say, "I love you," and, "You are important to me," to the ones you love every chance you get. Grief at the final parting is much cleaner if those words have not been left unsaid.

MY WALK THROUGH the dying time continued over a roller-coaster-ride year. In late March, with my wedding date set little more than six months later on September 21, I discovered that my adored aunt Cathy had been diagnosed with stage four non-Hodgkin's lymphoma. Sixty years old, a former smoker for twenty years, and a chronic dieter who had gained and lost the same forty pounds more times than I could count, my aunt's chances for beating this disease were slim. Although she sounded positive and ready to fight the good fight, I hung up the phone after hearing her news, got in the shower, and cried for a long time beneath the sound of the water.

Knowing how quickly things could change with this disease, I was anxious to visit her and drove up the first weekend in June, which corresponded with a "good week" for her, between heavy chemotherapy treatments.

I arrived—my first visit in more than a year—to find my aunt looking much older and wearing a baseball cap on her balding head. My uncle Marshall seemed much older too, bent and stooped from a second, unsuccessful back operation. I suddenly had the sensation that life was flashing by at whirlwind speed.

How grateful I was, then, to have had that wonderful weekend with my aunt while she was still enjoying some quality of life. We shared long, animated conversations and delicious dinners, and we celebrated Marshall's seventy-sixth birthday together. Before leaving, I gave my aunt a gift she could enjoy during the following week of treatments: a six-video set of the recent BBC adaptation of *Pride and Prejudice*, complete with Colin Firth as the best ever Mr. Darcy and the luminous Jennifer Ehle portraying Miss Elizabeth Bennett. Aunt Cathy called the day after I'd returned home to tell me she'd watched almost the whole thing in one afternoon, and it was making her difficult week more bearable.

Back in Nashville, my week was getting worse. My beloved Akita, Jojo, needed surgery, which entailed a whirlwind trip to Knoxville, more than three hours away, to an orthopedic specialist at the Veterinary Teaching Hospital at the University of Tennessee.

Early in July, as Jojo's cast came off and we were beginning diligent aftercare, my aunt crashed during her last chemotherapy treatments, suffered a stroke, and was admitted to the intensive care unit at Decatur Memorial Hospital, where she would remain for two months. As soon as I could leave Jojo, I was on the road again, back to my aunt's house in Warrensburg where cousin Andrea was now home between college and graduate school, keeping intense hospital vigils along with her father.

I was not prepared, just one month after my last visit, for the dramatic change in my aunt's appearance. I walked into her room in ICU and into a new chapter of the dying time, one that plays out daily in hospitals all over the world, a chapter no one asks for or hopes to experience. The combination of radical chemo treatments and blood-thinning medications required after her stroke had left my beautiful aunt Cathy hairless and eerily gaunt. Her eyes had a wild, desperate look, and she was hooked up to more monitors and IV tubes than seemed humane.

Though the treatments were over, there was no guarantee of remission. The new battle for her seemed to be making it through the day and night, and then the next day and night, in hopes of eventually feeling like living again.

The intensive care ward became a brave new world for the uninitiated, where the fine lines between life and death become infinitely thinner. My cousin Andrea and I sat at the nurses' station outside Cathy's room, talked about life and death, and watched similar dramas play out in other rooms up and down the floor of that hospital. We heard whispered conversations take place between doctors and relatives, out of the patient's hearing: "If she codes [slang for 'code blue'], you will have to decide whether to resuscitate." "Do you think she can get better?" "What if she still has cancer?" "Can she survive another stroke?"

My prayers changed by the second as my aunt suffered five cardiac arrests over the next two days. "God, please save her. Lord, I don't even know what to pray . . . I pray for mercy . . ."

Then I accepted my aunt's fragile hold on life with grim clarity. As Aunt Lois had done with Uncle Huby, I learned to embrace the dying time and wrap myself around all that was happening. There were phone calls, comings and goings of the family, and vigils—like the night of the first cardiac arrest when Andrea and I, afraid to leave, stayed all night in Aunt Cathy's room, thanks to the floor nurses who stretched visiting rules.

I knew she could die at any moment, but she was holding on for a last good-bye to her brother. I told my father this as I met him at the Decatur airport and drove to the hospital. Though it was midnight and he must have been exhausted, my father had prepared to face the circumstances. He stood close to his sister on the right side of her bed, with Andrea on the other side, and me at the end, my hands on Cathy's feet. Then my father surpassed all expectations for a reassuring bedside manner, talking normally, exhibiting no sign of awkwardness or distress over her alarming appearance. Cathy looked at her brother, her daughter, and then me, and said, "This is special." I felt a soft, warm presence envelop us in the room at that moment and marveled silently at a peacefulness and comfort that seemed touchable.

But a peaceful death was not to be. My aunt's eyes rolled back, lights flashed, alarms sounded, and another cardiac arrest flung the room into chaos. We moved into the hall, making way for the nurses and doctors. Andrea was in hysterics, my father looked distressed and shocked, and I was convinced Cathy was giving up her struggle.

Not so, a calm patient counselor came minutes later with the miraculous news. Cathy was still with us.

My father settled in for a lengthy stay a few days later as I left for Nashville on the renewed hope that my aunt might actually survive this. Daily responsibilities called me home— a record album in progress, a book contract pending, my wedding being planned. I never expected that during a close call with one dying time another crisis could be brewing.

IN NASHVILLE JOJO, now four weeks out from knee surgery, had gone into a mysterious decline. He had not eaten for days, even after my return, and his weight was down by at least ten pounds. He seemed listless and depressed. Alarmed into quick action, I loaded him into the van and headed back to Knoxville, anticipating a complication with the recent knee surgery.

The internist, Dr. Anderson, told me what I couldn't believe—an initial diagnosis of lymphoma. Possibly facing the same terminal disease as my aunt Cathy, Jojo was immediately checked into intensive care. I made the long drive back to Nashville in misery. Alternately weeping and praying, I knew I had to confront the dying times. I felt mortality closing in on me and, with this reality, leaned into God. There was nothing else to do, I decided, but keep leaning harder.

My days hung on regular phone calls from Knoxville and from Illinois. From Knoxville I was relieved to learn Jojo had tested negative for lymphoma. He wasn't out of the woods yet, but after some treatments for what turned out to be Addison's disease, he had returned to eating and was roaming around the veterinary ICU, checking out the other animals. I was jubilant, along with Dr. Anderson, who took Jojo to visit all the ICU shifts and show the students that sometimes the critical patients do recover.

By mid-August Jojo was home again, gaining weight and enjoying his status as miracle dog, my book contract was signed, Aunt Cathy—though still in the hospital—had been moved out of intensive care, and my wedding plans were progressing. Not a day passed during this time that I didn't feel humble and grateful for every facet of life. At age thirty-nine, I was on the verge of being married for the first time and anticipating a new creative outlet—a book deal that seemed to have been handed to me as a gift from God. This was a time when it seemed I walked a tiny tightrope between life and death, above chasms of the horrible and beautiful. I had a sense for every moment of life that the dying time especially heightens, a newfound wonder for it all.

TO THIS DAY I'm amazed at the providence surrounding my wedding date, September 21. John and I enjoyed a carefree celebration framed on either side by the drama of the dying time.

In October, as the post-wedding dust settled, I planned a short weekend visit to see my aunt, who was finally home from the hospital but confined to a special bed set up in the living room of her house in Warrensburg.

Cathy looked so much better than when I had seen her in the intensive care unit in July. About an inch of dark, baby-soft hair capped her head. She had primped for my arrival and was wearing a touch of her signature blue eye shadow and pink lipstick. There was a translucent quality to her porcelain skin. Thinner than she had been in twenty years, my aunt reminded me now of the way she looked when I first laid eyes on her more than thirty years earlier—except for an eerie calmness behind her eyes I did not want to recognize.

Despite the hospital bed set up in the living room, and the frequent hovering of the nurse my uncle had hired, this visit unfolded as just a continuation of the long, easy relationship I'd always had with my aunt Cathy. The joy of seeing her at home, far away from the nightmare of the ICU, helped push troubling signs to the back of my mind. I was hoping to push the dying time beyond arm's length. But Cathy's usually robust appetite for food was greatly diminished. She barely ate enough to keep a bird alive, and her emotional fragility surfaced more frequently and powerfully. We would be in the middle of an animated discussion, when a chance phrase would set off a wave of depression. I watched in amazement as sadness convulsed her face, bringing tears, and then disappeared into placid remoteness before I could complete a gesture of comfort. I was reluctant to acknowledge this as the natural course for a terminally ill patient.

Instead, I clung to moments of reassurance that things would be like they always were for us. The night before I left, the three of us, Cathy, Marshall, and I, had a cozy bedside dinner and conversation that felt like old times. My aunt seemed completely herself that night, witty and charming, sitting up in her bed and gesturing with her hands to make a point, just as she'd always done. I thought, *She's going to make it through this after all.*

By the next morning, though, as I quickly shared a few wedding pictures before heading back to Nashville, Aunt Cathy was subdued and remote once more. The words I could not say hung between us. *Are you dying? What do you think about in the middle of the night? Is this the last time we will be together? Have I told you what it has meant to me all these years, having you for my favorite aunt?*

I wanted to encourage her to drink more water, eat more, move her body around. As a wellness professional, having supplemented my musician's income for many years working as a personal fitness trainer, I knew these things could help people feel better. Yet I felt awkward voicing such instructions. Who was I to tell my aunt, who had gone to hell and back in the past six months, what to do at this point? My intuition told me I might never see her again, but my heart held onto hope. *Maybe she will regain her strength and will to live. Maybe the cancer is in remission and we will have more time.*

I didn't want to feel the gulf that stretched between us, even as I held her hand in mine—I, newly married, looking forward to the second half of my life, and my aunt, making a life transition I couldn't share with her. Finally, I attempted to bridge the canyon. "I can't begin to understand the way you feel right now," I started. "I haven't been through what you have these past months, but try to remember what you love about life. Remember how good it feels to sit down to Thanksgiving dinner, how beautiful the first snowfall looks on the ground, how wonderful it is to walk outside without a jacket in the spring and feel the warm air against your skin. Think about your dogs and your daughter and all the people who love you . . . like I love you."

It was a clumsy gesture I had to make, and we both knew it, a barely veiled plea to my aunt: Please, please, don't give up on life.

As I drove away, I could see her perfect profile through the big bay window of the living room. She was propped up by the pillows in her bed, and from this perspective looked suddenly like herself as a young woman. Only I knew she really was dying.

LESS THAN A WEEK later, my aunt was admitted into the hospital again. I called to say I was on my way, quickly packing enough clothes for several days, including black for a funeral.

As I drove that much loved route a fourth time in six months, I was drenched with more emotion than I could name, a bizarre combination of grief, nostalgia, and a strange exhilaration for being alive. It's a knife's-edge place between living and dying, and a place where every sense seems enhanced. The landscape is clearer, the music on the radio more beautiful, the feeling of the air on your skin more exquisite. And it's interesting that these beautiful things can mingle with the horrible.

When I reached the hospital and rushed to her room, my aunt was still alive but unconscious. Her mouth gaped open as her whole body labored to breathe. Later, as her breaths came farther and farther apart, it was as though the four of us—Marshall, Andrea, Aunt Cathy, and I—were finishing a long journey that had been inevitable since the first diagnosis.

"She is leaving us," I said, holding one of her hands. Andrea held the other, and Marshall had his hands on her feet.

I sat by my aunt's right side and read aloud from the Bible I'd brought with me, her favorite selections from Psalm 121: "The LORD is your keeper; the LORD is your shade at your right hand. The sun shall not strike you by day, nor the moon by night."

A soft, thick presence seemed to surround us. It was the same soft completeness I had sensed that night three months ago in the ICU after my father had arrived. As my aunt breathed out her last breath, I read, "The LORD shall preserve you from all evil; He shall preserve your soul." The warm, comforting presence left the room. The machines hummed louder, and I knew Aunt Cathy's spirit had gone back to God. "The LORD shall preserve your going out and your coming in from this time forth and even forevermore."

WHILE I HAVE NEVER heard God speak audibly to me and have often felt spiritually lacking when some Christians describe such an experience, the transcendent moment when my aunt Cathy died convinces me that God sometimes uses a language stronger than words. That moment was so real I could have physically leaned into it and been held up in place. Aunt Cathy's spirit was lovingly met, then escorted from her physical body to a place I cannot see but believe to be heaven.

My aunt's gentle passing considerably lightened the burden of fear I'd always associated with death. For while the grief of loss remains, it is not a hopeless grief. Frederick Buechner describes this so well in his book *The Magnificent Defeat.* Life is like the bird, he writes, that flies in through one window of a large castle to bat about wildly for a brief period of time, then out through another window and gone.

How wonderful life is in the joy of those first flights, all that promise lying in a new beginning. How tenaciously we embrace the drama played out in the large castle rooms of our short, human stories. How tempting it is to want to dance there as long as we can, far away from the inevitable exit, the other window. Yet how profoundly beautiful that exit can be—a different kind of birth, a deliverance from the frailties and limitations of our humanness, the ultimate freedom of our spirit, returning to the God who gave it (see Eccles. 12:7).

I reel in sorrow from every loss I've suffered and I weep in anticipation of the losses to come. But I celebrate the gift of that second window—and the horrible/beautiful dying time—knowing an exquisite reunion awaits each one of us as we wing our way home to God.

five

Dream Sojourn

Missing Diana

I have to remind myself some birds aren't meant to be caged. Their feathers are just too bright. And when they fly away, the part of you that knows it was a sin to lock them up does rejoice. But still, the place you live is that much more drab and empty that they're gone.

RED IN FRANK DARABONT'S
THE SHAWSHANK REDEMPTION SCREENPLAY,
BASED ON A STEPHEN KING NOVELLA

MY IMAGINATION AS A CREATIVE being has always been pulled in the direction of dreams. I used to dream of escaping my crowded family house, having a place, a space, and an identity uniquely my own. I dreamed of one day meeting the perfect man who would live up to all my expectations and be the right one to go with me through life, happily ever after. I've dreamed of setting violin bow to violin strings and being magical, of becoming rich and famous and sought after, standing on stages and hearing in the roar of applause the affirmation that I am finally enough.

I've dreamed perfect dreams of fairy tales coming true.

Is that so wrong?

ON LABOR DAY WEEKEND 1997 I set out on the road to Decatur, feeling unusually reticent about the journey ahead. It was only the second time I'd made this trip since Aunt Cathy had died the previous fall, and I was in the middle of one of those periods of life when it seemed as though there was more to beat me down than lift me up.

Instead of enjoying the drive north, I succumbed to the loathsome exercise of listing the many reasons for my discontent with life. My habit during such negative thinking includes imagining all the other things that could possibly go wrong. *What if I have an accident? What if my car breaks down? What if . . . ?*

I was on a mission after all. I'd promised Uncle Marshall that I'd take Aunt Cathy's elderly, untrained, much-loved pair of collies back with me to Nashville to live out the remainder of their lives. It was time to make good on that promise, though I could find little consolation in this noble action. I couldn't help picturing myself, stranded on the side of the road halfway between Decatur and Nashville, in the midst of the heat and traffic of this holiday weekend, with two full-size collies in the back of my van.

I'd made the offer in the days immediately following my aunt's death, as we wondered how my uncle was going to get along without Cathy. He must have wondered himself. "This wasn't the way we'd planned it," he said. "I was supposed to die first." And in a statement that spoke volumes about their marriage—not to mention his idea of which was the weaker sex—he'd added, "It's much better for a man to die and leave the woman behind than the other way around, because a woman knows how to take care of herself."

Marshall had suffered for some time with ailments that left him physically limited—back pain, muscle weakness, arthritis. It was hard for him to take care of the large house and yard, located at the edge of Warrensburg, across the highway from acres of corn and soybean fields, now tended by tenant farmers. He was especially worried about looking after the dogs, and it was during one of his particularly grim-sounding musings that he'd mumbled something to the effect of "finding a humane situation for the collies." I spoke the words without thinking: "Maybe I could take them . . ."

I regretted those words almost as soon as they were out of my mouth, but there was no turning back. My uncle fastened onto the idea with gusto. It was the perfect solution to the problem as far as he was concerned. Cathy, he said, would be so happy to know that I took those dogs.

"Those dogs" were in fact my aunt's pride and joy. She had owned and bred Lassie-style, English collies for nearly twenty-five years. At the time of her death, she had a male tricolor named Mozart, who might have been her all-time favorite dog; and his mate, a sable-colored female named Sugar. They were a beautiful pair and inseparable as a long-married collie couple, having lived in each other's shadow for more than eight years. But they weren't housebroken and, in my opinion, were dumber than bricks. It would be difficult to place even one of them in a new home.

My own delight in furry creatures (I've owned plenty), and my own soft heart for the plight of strays (which seem to have a special antenna for finding me) are pleasant passions I shared with my aunt Cathy. But I already had four dogs at home, and of all the breeds in the world I would never have anticipated owning, voluminously haired, needle-nosed collies would top the list. Nevertheless, I had made a promise, and even in the face of inevitable hassles ahead, I felt it was the right thing to do.

The visit with my uncle, who lived alone now with his aches and loneliness, was emotionally draining. We rattled around the big house in Warrensburg, trying to find a new rhythm without Cathy. I couldn't sit at the kitchen table without imagining my aunt leaning against the counter to fix dinner, the upper half of her body turned toward me, as she chatted and her hands operated on autopilot.

Marshall had regular help now, a woman who came in during the week to cook and clean for him, drive him to doctor appointments, and so forth, and the house was more barrenly neat than I'd ever seen it. In the past, the pantry off the kitchen always had shelves stuffed to overflowing with canned and packaged goods, cooking and laundering paraphernalia, and mountains of dog supplies. Now it was nearly empty. Pristine rows of these items lined the shelves in antiseptic organization. The place was so tidy it might have been a picture of someone's dream home out of a magazine.

But beautiful as the house was in this state, I ached for the comforting disarray of my aunt's careless housekeeping.

MY PLAN WAS TO DRIVE back to Nashville on Sunday, avoiding the throngs that would invariably be on the road Labor Day itself. So, waking early on August 31, a beautiful, peaceful morning, I retrieved the Decatur *Herald & Review* from one of the stone pillars at either side of the driveway, where the paper boy always left it, and went back into the house to eat breakfast and drink a cup of coffee. There would be time after reading the news, I decided, to load up the collies and say goodbye to my uncle.

Then I opened the newspaper at the kitchen table, and along with the rest of the world, gasped at the huge, black letters that filled the headline: PRINCESS DIANA, DEAD.

I couldn't believe it. The news shocked and dismayed me much as would the sudden death of a person I knew intimately. And then, with the strange ability humans have to temporarily tuck aside something unbearably sad in order to complete a task at hand—with an implicit understanding that the feelings would be honored in due course—I tore my attention away from the story coming out of Paris where the accident had occurred and set about getting on the road. I knew if I lingered over the paper or turned on the television, I'd be there for hours.

I said good-bye to my uncle, barely concealing my impatience. But Marshall, after months of reminding me to come and get them, was now struggling with his emotions over letting go of the collies—such strong, living, breathing connections to his beloved wife.

Endings, I was reminded, are rarely storybook in fashion.

Barely out of the driveway and onto the street, I flipped the radio tuner, scanning the airwaves for the latest on Diana's death. For the next six and a half hours, I listened in shock to the news bulletins coming in from around the world, driving, weeping, and trying to absorb the unfathomable fact that this young woman, four years my junior, was suddenly gone. As with previous experiences of outliving people I never imagined I'd outlive, I felt oddly vulnerable and immortal. It reminded me that anything can happen to anyone at anytime. And yet I was alive, fully, powerfully alive, barreling down the highway in an old Mazda van with two distracting dogs in the back, while somewhere in Paris, Princess Diana was lying in a hospital room, cold and dead. *How does the most famous, privileged, protected woman in the world die in a car crash?* I wondered. *How is it that this thirty-six-year-old princess, four years younger than I, died on this holiday weekend, while I, just an obscure, unprotected, unprivileged person, am still alive?*

I cried so much on the long road home that I thought my tears were spent by the time I finally pulled into our driveway. As soon as I greeted my husband, though, feeling safe in the haven of our unspectacular life, I started weeping again. I said to my husband, "How can I feel so sad for this woman I never met, a person who wouldn't have known to shed tears for me?"

But I did feel so sad, as though something special to the world had been taken away and that we were all the poorer for the loss.

I wasn't alone. One of my neighbors told me she got up at 4 A.M. the day Diana's funeral was broadcast on live TV in Nashville. As we commiserated over the loss of "our Princess," she told me how she'd noticed the glow of television sets all up and down the street, breaking the early-morning darkness.

FIVE YEARS LATER, at the risk of sounding like a woman with too much time on her hands, I have to say, I still miss Princess Diana. I miss the sight of her beautiful face, with its mix of strong and delicate features that were truly beautiful because they transcended the trite, stereotypical prettiness. I miss glancing at the tabloid covers while waiting in the checkout line at the grocery store and rolling my eyes at her latest scrape or scandal. I miss seeing her on television, harnessing her megawatt celebrity to unpopular charitable causes and daring us not to see and feel the plight of the human condition as she did. As much as I deplore the cheap, celebrity-ism that engulfs our culture, I admit the sight or mention of the Princess of Wales always gave me pleasure.

I guess, like so many women I know, my irrational feelings of connection to Diana trace back to the early days of her courtship with Prince Charles. I can remember exactly where I was at the time of their royal wedding (of course, I was glued to the television). Out of Juilliard for two years, feeling like a failure in every area of my life, I sat in the living room of my almost affianced, but never-to-be-married-to, boyfriend and watched this luminescent twenty-year-old as she fulfilled the childhood dream of every girl, to grow up and marry Prince Charming.

I remember watching her climb out of the horse-drawn carriage, her attendants adjusting the miles-long train of her gown, looking like a vision straight out of a fairy tale. I envied her with every bone in my body. I thought: *She is the luckiest woman in the world. She is marrying the handsome, if weak-chinned, Prince. She will be rich and admired. She'll dress up in beautiful clothes and lead a charmed life.* And, what seemed to me at the time as most enviable of all: *She will never have to wonder about what to do with her life.*

Time would tell a different story.

Diana wasn't the luckiest woman in the world, and she did not live a charmed life. Her prince, who didn't love her, turned out to be an admitted adulterous frog. Perhaps with the exception of almost always being perfectly coifed, Diana struggled with the same issues that haunt most every woman I know: low self-esteem, disappointment in marriage or relationships, depression, romantic betrayals, disordered eating, a sense of fracturedness or frenzy in trying to play too many roles too well, no real solid sense of her true identity.

Yet, amazingly, by playing out all her failings in the glare of public scrutiny, Diana became only more princess-like. Though so vulnerable and so flawed—flawed fatally, it turned out—she seemed to possess some transparent hope that life could hold beauty and happiness and love.

This higher view seemed to develop especially in the year before her death. Diana seemed to have come to terms with the reality of her situation—divorce, emotional disgrace, honest disappointment in herself and others. In her acceptance of imperfection, she achieved an apparent enjoyment of what life still had to offer. A photo spread for *Vanity Fair* magazine captured this. I bought that issue of the magazine for the single purpose of soaking in the beauty of those photographs, which show Diana shortly before auctioning her gowns for charity. The woman in the pictures radiates a relaxed peacefulness that cannot be manufactured by lighting, makeup, hairstyling, or the mastery of retouch artists. I remember thinking to myself: *She has finally become comfortable inside her own skin.* And then: *She looks translucent, almost too exquisite to be of this world.*

Such is the transforming power of hanging your dreams not on a star but inside yourself.

A FRIEND ONCE SAID to me, "It's as desolate to live only in dreams as it is to have no dreams at all." In the continuum between those two extremes, I've probably erred on the side of living too much in dreams. My relentless pursuit of them has brought many disappointments. Placing the violin bow on violin strings at the age of eight opened a Pandora's box of sorts, a long, love/hate relationship with an instrument that has alternately tortured and blessed me. Growing up and leaving my childhood home did not allow me to escape any detail of my history anymore than leaving classical music saved me the pain of coming to terms with my musical and career limitations. In marriage I've learned my husband has feet of clay as all men do, as do I; we've each learned how to plow through the terrible loneliness unique to marriage, when looking into the remoteness of each other's eyes, you can't understand how on earth you got to such a desolate place. As for finding fulfillment through the adulation of others, I've learned painfully and absolutely the inherent emptiness of that dream.

However, I've never tasted the dry dust of a dreamless life. I continue to dream—big dreams, fueled by the same reckless hope with which I embrace my faith, faith being "sure of what we hope for and certain of what we do not see" (Heb. 11:1 NIV).

I have to believe that the mountaintop experiences I've been blessed with in the past are real and reliable enough to anticipate in my future. I can't live without hopes of fairy-tale proportion instilled in my heart. I know there will always be dreams that come true and other dreams that will never be realized. I've learned that some dreams don't come true, so others can. So I hold tightly in my soul the dreams that hang somewhere between the grit of reality and something big, blue-sky, and wild. I still hope the outpourings of my pen and violin will move audiences, I still dream of falling in and out of and back in love with my husband for the rest of my life, I still wish to buy back my great-grandparents' farm in Wisconsin, and I still hope to play for a state dinner at the White House one day.

These dreams are like brightly feathered birds too beautiful to be caged, or a lovely princess who could not be trapped under a crown or behind a moat, or the child bubbling to friends an unbridled fantasy. They are to be witnessed and touched and celebrated, brightening—if only for a season—an imperfect world.

six

Milestones

Unearthing Legacy

When you remember me, it means that you have carried something of who I am with you, that I have left some mark of who I am on who you are. . . . It means that even after I die, you can still see my face and hear my voice and speak to me in your heart. . . . For as long as you remember me, I am never entirely lost.

FREDERICK BUECHNER, *WHISTLING IN THE DARK*

I'VE OFTEN WONDERED how different my life might have been if I were named Kim or Susan or Jane. But I am Ruth, named after my father's mother, my grandmother, Ruth Nelson McGinnis. Along with her name I inherited a special antenna tuned into the drama of her early death at age forty-eight from breast cancer and my father's heavy, unresolved sadness linked to the way he lost her.

That antenna was so tuned in to fear that by age thirteen I had a morbid fascination with breast cancer and spent hours poring over descriptions of mastectomies in our family medical journal and checking my own barely developed breasts for lumps. That antenna also included a sense of obligation to wear my grandmother's name well. Often my father spoke of his mother, as if to remind me of what I had missed by not knowing her. So I understood from a young age that she had been special and that bearing her name was a privilege.

It's taken me years, and many trips to my grandmother's grave site, to make peace with her legacy. For years I knew only how inevitably our imperfect lives are shaped by the imperfect people we've never met.

GREENWOOD CEMETERY LIES QUIETLY beside Highway 35, just outside of Superior, Wisconsin. A few miles south the same road leads to the dramatic waterfalls of Pattison State Park, but this old cemetery has its own beauty. It's aptly named, filled with green grass and towering pines. Bordered by the highway in front and railroad tracks in back, it's a peaceful place, even with the mournful whistle and chugging sounds of an occasional passing train. Names like Hanson, Anderson, Larson, and Olson are etched into the gravestones, reflecting the concentration of Scandinavian immigrants who settled in this northern tip of Wisconsin. They were sturdy, hardworking people who thrived here despite the brutal, long winters.

The sun is shining brightly on this early spring day, though dirty drifts of snow remain in the shaded areas, a reminder that winter has not yet surrendered. The graveyard is empty, so I'm grateful for the companionship of JoJo. He's basking in the sunshine, no doubt grateful to be out of his traveling crate for a while.

I sit in front of a plain, flat, granite marker, one of twenty-some thousand graves in this quiet place, a stone so small and unassuming that, even knowing its location, you could walk right by it. But this grave is significant to me, enough to have traveled here from Nashville three times to find it. Resting in this family plot are my father's maternal grandparents, an uncle, and his mother, Ruth.

I have pulled handfuls of encroaching grass away from her stone, as I did the last time I was here. The ground has long since obscured the gravestones to the left, where her parents, Great-Grandpa and Grandma Nelson, are buried. I was so relieved to have found her stone, relieved that the ground and grass had not erased her presence as well, for no one had tended this grave for a very long time.

While rambling about the Wisconsin hometowns of my parents several years ago, I made the startling discovery that my father and his two younger sisters had never come back to this place after their mother was buried. That trip was the first time I had visited these places as an adult, a unique trip taken with my parents, youngest sister, two aunts, and cousins. While visiting the farmlands around Menomonie, where my mother grew up, we had stopped by the graves of her parents and grandparents and even visited a cemetery where her mother's extended family rests. As our journey continued north to my father's boyhood town of Superior, I eagerly anticipated visiting the grave of my namesake.

We had stayed overnight after spending a pleasant afternoon driving around the neighborhoods where my father was born and raised. The next morning, on the way out of town, we pulled into Greenwood Cemetery. As we began what would be a fruitless search, I was stunned to hear my father say that he hadn't been here since he was seventeen, not since the day that his mother was buried.

Our visit was an exercise in futility; we might as well have been looking for a needle in a haystack. Though I was

stubbornly determined, my father seemed increasingly reticent about finding his mother's grave. His relief was pal-
pable as we abandoned our efforts and drove away, on to a
family wedding in Minneapolis, away from graveyards and
the past. I was disappointed but finally accepted that even
after so many years, facing his mother's grave was still painful
for my father. I found comfort in knowing that I would come
back to this place one day.

A year and a half later, I made the trip again, this time on
my own terms. I was determined to find my grandmother's
grave. After hours of searching, I finally made my way to an
office across the highway I hadn't known existed, fortuitously
guided there by the only other person visiting the graveyard
that day. "I am looking for my grandmother's grave," I said.
"She was buried here in 1948, next to her father, Fred Nelson. No one has visited her in a very long time; no one in my
family knows where she rests."

After the kind woman in the office directed me to the right
lot and block number, the grave was easy to spot: "Ruth Nelson McGinnis 1899–1948." Seeing my first and last name on
that flat piece of granite hit me hard, like an eerie prophecy.
Now, as then, it is sobering, a reminder of the mixed blessing
this woman's name and legacy have etched into my life.

WE ARE SURELY A PART of everywhere we've been, and I believe
we are a part of the long, human drama that precedes us. Our

lives are inevitably shaped by people we have never met, especially in family lines. So it has been with my connection to my grandmother Ruth. Though she died nine years before I was born, her abbreviated life and sad dying time has imprinted my heart and psyche as tangibly as the name on her gravestone.

My grandmother's early death was the defining moment in the lives of my father and his younger sisters, my aunts Marian and Cathy. It is as though the pain of her passing were frozen, then sealed in their respective hearts; my father was seventeen, Marian fifteen, and Cathy just twelve. Fifty years after her mother's death, my aunt Marian describes the day of the burial in exquisite, painful detail: "She died in October. The trees were bare, the skies were overcast, and at the cemetery the wind blew dry leaves across the ground. When they lowered her coffin into the ground, I shivered, and my stomach felt like a big, heavy lump inside of me."

Sitting in the sun, I have to close my eyes to imagine that desolate scene—the sad group gathered in this place, bundled against the cold, grieving for the loss of Ruth Nelson McGinnis. Her three children, standing here pinched and pale, experienced the death of their mom in separate realities. My father had known for two years that his mother was slowly dying. His father had confided in him one night, while they were out in the shed behind the house, candling eggs for their egg delivery business. Marian had been warned six months in advance to prepare for this day, when early that spring, after Sunday school and before Sunday dinner, her father took her for a drive, south of town: "Your mother isn't going to get well, Marian. When she had the operation four years ago, they found cancer. She is going to die. And I want you to act the same as always. Don't let her know that you know."

Cathy, the youngest, had no warning at all. Her mother had been in the hospital for many weeks when the next-door neighbor came to the door one morning to deliver the sad news that their mother had died.

I imagine them standing around this grave—my father dry-eyed and stoic; Marian heartbroken, struggling to understand why it had to be her mom; Cathy in a state of shocked disbelief. A bleak October day . . . a gaping hole in the ground . . . the sound of dirt hitting the coffin . . . reddened, tear-streaked faces . . . immense sadness over the lost life of this gentle, gifted woman, the grandmother I never met.

SHE WAS THE YOUNGEST of five children born to my great-grandparents, Frederick and Britta (Betty) Nelson, Scandinavian immigrants who met and married in America in 1891, after growing up not fifty miles away from each other in Sweden. Fred and Betty had great ambitions for their children, managing to put them all through college, an unusual achievement in those times. The four sisters—Ruth, Esther, Ethel, and Vi—shared a close relationship their whole lives, staying in touch with frequent letters after Esther married and moved to Montana, and Vi married and moved away to Shawano,

Wisconsin. Ethel married last and was widowed after seven years, eventually moving in with their mother, Great-Grandma Nelson, who lived to be ninety-five. The apartment they shared in Duluth, Minnesota, was only a short bus or car ride away from Ruth and her family in Superior and became a refuge for my father and his sisters after their mom passed away.

Although all the Nelson girls were quite accomplished, my grandmother Ruth was considered the "phoenix of the family," according to her sisters. It seems there was nothing she did not do and do brilliantly. She was an avid reader, belonging to book clubs, and a talented teacher, quietly subduing and then earning the cooperation and devotion of the class bully in my father's sixth-grade schoolroom. Ruth loved to write and sent stories to magazines in the hope of being published. She played both the piano and violin and encouraged her children to play music as well, an experience that surely encouraged my father to introduce his own children to music.

Over the years of childhood, I became acquainted with Ruth through my aunts and great-aunts. I heard about her sweet tooth (which I have inherited), her gentle, quick sense of humor, her brilliance, and her Victorian modesty. I would take all of this in and consider it carefully, even contemplating from time to time that I had been sadly deprived in never knowing her. But it was hard for me to feel regretful for too long, because I loved my step-grandmother Eva so very much.

IT WASN'T UNTIL I turned seventeen that I began to identify the legacy of pain my grandmother's death had etched into my father's life, and so into my own. As I became the age he was when his mother lay dying in the hospital, my father pulled out a yellowed, two-page letter she had written in pencil, now faded, on my father's seventeenth birthday, September 24, 1948. With twenty-three days of life remaining, her letter was deceptively calm, even cheerful. But, after warm birthday wishes to her eldest child and only son, came poignant lines of advice, clearly meant as counsel for a future she knew she would be unable to share.

"Be a grand man like your dad," she wrote. "Learn to do something you enjoy to do and learn it well." Then, most revealing of her own situation: "And don't forget to enjoy the wonderful things all around you."

I stood there, reading these words for the first time, straining to imagine what they had meant to my father when he was my age. He had honored me by allowing me to read this deathbed letter, and I was moved. When I looked up, I was astonished to see my father's eyes brimming with tears, as though his mother had died just weeks, instead of decades, earlier. Before I could think of anything to say, my mother walked into the room, and I was grateful for the interruption. It was the first time I had seen in my father's eyes the raw pain caused by my grandmother's death. I was emotionally unprepared for this departure from his usual stoic, though easygoing, personality.

I DIDN'T DWELL on my grandmother's short life or the circumstances surrounding her death again until I was in my late thirties. Then a series of events prodded me to revisit the legacy of my namesake. While writing my first book, I found myself interested in the farming background of my mother's side of the family, which renewed my interest in my father's side as well. That same year, my dad's youngest sister, my beloved aunt Cathy, was diagnosed with terminal non-Hodgkin's lymphoma, prompting me to make several trips to my hometown in Illinois to spend precious time with her. My aunt, though reluctant to reveal that she knew she was very sick, was frankly forthcoming with her life's memories, as the terminally ill often are. These memories, of course, revolved around that pivotal event in her life, the loss of her mom when she was only twelve years old.

Aunt Cathy, who always had a quick, irreverent sense of humor, had talked with me before about what life was like without her mother. The most often repeated story was about having to buy her first bra, on her own. She described going to the department store in Superior by herself, hoping desperately that she wouldn't run into anyone she knew, and buying the smallest bra she could find without even trying it on. Then she went home and hid it at the bottom of her underwear drawer until she worked up the courage to wear it. Her account of this adolescent enterprise always made me smile.

My aunt talked about how stunned and angry she, Marian, and my dad had been when their newly widowed father started dating another woman and remarried within the year. Their lives, already turned upside down, were disrupted once more as Eva (the new stepmother) wisely chose to begin her marriage in a new house away from the many reminders of Ruth's tragic absence.

It was, according to Aunt Cathy, the lifesaving trips across Lake Superior to visit Aunt Ethel and Grandma Nelson in their cozy apartment in Duluth that helped them through a difficult time. There they would eat King Gustafs cookies and homemade rolls, drink Grandma Nelson's thick coffee laced with lots of milk and sugar, and pour out all their woes. Shortly before Aunt Cathy died, she wrote that Grandma Nelson "always stuck up for me. . . . She became my mother after mother died. I adored her."

CATHY DIED LATER that year. Though grief stricken over losing my favorite aunt, I found some comfort in the thought of her finally being with her mother. For my father and Aunt Marian, having to part with their youngest sibling was especially wrenching, triggering old memories of loss.

The unresolved pain of my grandmother's death rose up like a familiar tide. As friends and family gathered after Cathy's funeral, my aunt Marian leaned against the kitchen counter in her sister's house and compared the scene to the one she remembered nearly fifty years earlier, when their mother had died.

"It was just like this, the house crowded with people I'd never seen before," she said, "sitting in my mama's living room, eating, chattering, laughing. I wanted them all to go home."

As I listened to my aunt Marian speak these words with fresh pain in her voice, I was struck again by the enduring tragedy of my grandmother's death. It puzzled me then, and puzzles me now, that Ruth's passing, half a century old, has never retreated to that natural place of bittersweet memory and acceptance. Though questions remain, I have found some answers in bits and pieces of my grandmother's life excavated through stubborn curiosity: a stash of old pictures of Ruth found at my aunt's house after she died; a priceless stack of letters that my grandmother wrote to my great aunt Esther, most of them from 1948, saved from the trash heap by my cousin Debbie; finally, a journal kept by my great aunt Vi (shared with me by her son) from that same, poignant year. Together these treasures have opened a window into the heart and life of my grandmother Ruth, revealing more of her than I could ever have gleaned from the descriptions passed down by my father and his sisters.

ONE OF THE EARLIEST pictures I have of my grandmother is from her eighth grade graduation. She is standing with eight other girls, all in Victorian white lace dresses with serious expressions on their faces, gathered around an even more serious-looking schoolmaster. Another graduation portrait, probably from high school, shows her as a young woman with a soft, dreamy look in her eyes. A family picture taken in the 1920s shows the whole Nelson family, Fred and Betty sitting in front of their five handsome children; my very good-looking great-uncle Wally standing behind them, a pair of Nelson sisters on either side.

My favorite pictures are those taken early in my grandmother's marriage. In one she holds my father as an infant, bundled up against a cold, though sunny, day. In another, Ruth looks on as Great-Grandma Nelson holds the baby in her lap, sitting in the backyard on a breezy but warmer day. I can see from these pictures that Ruth loved being a mother. It was a role she yearned for but didn't experience until the age of thirty. She married later in life than planned. When he was twenty or so, my grandfather broke off their engagement on the advice of a Catholic aunt who was concerned that Ruth wasn't Catholic. Several years later, he saw Ruth walk out of a department store in Superior, and he decided that he was going to "marry that girl" after all.

I've often wondered how their breakup and long separation affected my grandmother. Living in the same small town, enduring the awkwardness of running into him at the store or the movie theater. Their wedding portrait shows no signs of that heartbreak, just a gently contented look on her face and in her soft, dreamy eyes.

There is one picture in my treasured collection I don't care to look at much. It's a stark, studio picture of my grandmother that must have been taken during her last years of life. Though only forty-six or forty-seven, she looks to be well into her sixties. She's wearing wire-rimmed glasses that obscure her eyes that I have grown to love. The slight smile on her mouth doesn't reach any other part of her face. This picture reflects the pain of her final years, an outward expression of an internal struggle barely revealed, even in her letters to her sister, my great-aunt Esther.

THE LETTERS HAVE BEEN a blessing. Handwritten in beautiful cursive script, or hammered out on a fussy typewriter (with a tendency to run out of ribbon), my grandmother's letters speak to me from beyond the grave. Her lively mind and heartfelt interest in others, her likes and dislikes leap off each page. In a letter dated January 31, 1929, she writes to her sister with joy over the birth of Esther's first son:

I'm so tickled, Esther and Homer! Somehow I always hoped it would be a boy. Hope someone writes or has written, to tell us everything: Whom he resembles and gee! What's his name?

A letter from September 4, 1939, celebrates the birth of Esther's third and last child, a second son. By now Ruth has a family of her own and writes:

Now you are at the stage where you are simply enjoying the luxury of loafing, aren't you? I always loved the nice long rest and the tray of food at mealtime. And the thrill of having the baby brought to you.

She goes on to describe her new roomer for the school term: "a nice ordinary chap—tall, red-headed and smiley," and writes how she will get a dollar a week for feeding him breakfast and ten dollars a month for the room. She comments on the shocking war news, Hitler's invasion of Poland: "It made me so nervous and heartsick the first day when it was all starting. If we have the sense we were born with, we'll surely keep out of it." Then she gives an account of canning food, part of the normal daily round for her, that is unimaginable to me. Her descriptions of the soul-satisfying labors of the homemaker in that time fill me with humble admiration, as I could no more accomplish such tasks than flap my arms and fly to the moon.

A letter dated December 12, 1942, is the last written before the breast surgery she endured in 1943. It describes a happy, busy, normal period of life, recounting her forty-second birthday celebration and preparations for Christmas:

I had a most pleasant birthday. Frank gave me a really handsome compact . . . a Yardley's, loose powder, with rouge paste, so it can be used for either lips or face. It is slim and long and fits nicely into my hand. Catherine gave me fingernail polish and a holder for the glass in the bedroom. We had a grand dinner at the Flame (a fancy dinner/dancing nightclub in Duluth). I had barbecued chicken, and for once it was a generous amount of chicken.

She closes this cheerful letter with the simple highlights of her normal life, describing Cathy's special part in the class Christmas party and new crisscross dotted swiss curtains she bought for the girls' room with her teaching money.

A letter written March 22, 1944, is less cheerful, relating the sudden and unexpected death of a close cousin, Cecil James Moe, the son of one of Great-Grandma Nelson's sisters. She describes the events leading up to Cecil's fatal heart attack at the age of forty-three, and with a beautiful ability to communicate details, she describes the throngs of visitors and what it was like to see family and friends they all knew but had not seen in years:

Alfred has a boy in Junior College, a girl in the Waves and one at St. Catherine's college. He is Alfred to a "T" but shrunken, thin-haired, and bug-eyed. . . . you'd know him in a minute, so trim and neat and very much himself. Bert is so much the old Bert that I was expecting his black and blue pinch momentarily. Is he fat! Is he full of how important his job is! And is he full of the dickens and old memories and stories! He made us all forget our trouble for stretches, all day.

At the end of this letter, she makes a glancing mention of her own health situation. "Had my last [radiation] treatment

137

today and it seems that if Dr. Sincock says it is all right I won't have to take the third one, which is what I hope."

THE REST OF MY GRANDMOTHER'S letters to her sister Esther, written in 1948, paint a heartrending account of the last nine months of her life. I can't help but think that the pathos of her dying time was intensified by the pretense surrounding her true condition. Cancer was suffered quietly in those days, typically hidden in shame. Still, the secrets within the family amaze me. Ruth's husband and son (my dad) had known she was dying for at least two years. But entries in Great-Aunt Vi's diary confirm that even her beloved sisters didn't know this until mid-March of the year that she died. In a tiny leather-bound "a line a day" diary, Vi writes:

> *March 15: Getting things ready for a St. Patrick's Day Party.*
> *March 16: Shopped all a.m. Went bowling. Headache kind of bad in eve.*
> *March 17: Ethel wrote about Ruth's fatal sickness. Sick at heart. Terrible headache all day.*
> *March 18: Called off St. Patrick's Party. Feel awful.*

I don't think my grandmother really knew the truth—that she was slowly dying of cancer—until that summer. A wonderful, long letter to Esther written on February 11 mentions nothing of her illness. Instead, it is filled with excitement (and sisterly reassurances) over Esther's eighteen-year-old daughter, Betty, suddenly engaged to be married. She writes that she would love to make the trip to Montana for the wedding, but it would depend on finances: "We feel very poor just now. Egg business is down to a minimum and living is so high. Really, all my spending money goes for food." She finishes this letter with a request for more details about the future son-in-law:

Write again soon. We still don't know: 1. His last name. 2. Have you met his folks? 3. Church? 4. Looks? We'd like a snap of him.

These queries bring a smile to my face. I can picture my grandmother, hunched over her typewriter, full of enthusiasm and interest over this big event in her sister's life.

The next letter to Esther, dated April 2, makes reference to what would be a steady theme in subsequent letters, that Ruth is losing her voice. A hint of anxiety creeps in between the lines.

I would like to be able to say what I long to say, that I'll be there with bells on. But I may not be able to make it. Here's why: I had the flu in February, and from then on I've had laryngitis and can scarcely talk yet. I feel well now except for a grinding worry over my voice, and an occasional nervous tension therefrom.

Still, by the end of this letter, she is hoping to make the trip to Montana and "dance at the wedding." "Keep your fingers crossed that my voice clears up, that the time works out, that the [doctor's] bill isn't too big, and I'll be seeing you."

A few weeks later, in a letter dated April 21, Ruth's voice has not improved, despite a series of medical treatments:

Oh boy, look at that date! I can imagine you are pretty busy and excited. I would surely love to go out, but I can't this time. All on account of my crazy old throat, which is still very bad, and my voice nothing to depend upon at all. My shots are done until [the doctor] gives me a check up to see what they have accomplished, if anything, and then I am supposed to have eleven more. I never dreamed that my health would be something to worry about, but there you are.

Now Ruth is hoping that Esther will make the trip east, after the wedding, for a nice long visit in Superior. And ever interested in the prospective son-in-law, she writes:

Gradually we're getting the "dope" on Keith. He sounds like a nice boy, and we like his looks, too. Tell me more about his job. What church does he go to? Does he have brothers and sisters? Funny to think you'll have another son. Imagine saying "my son-in-law." Gee Esther, where has all the time gone?

In her next letter, dated April 28, she's still convincing her sister to make the long visit: "Last evening and today I've taken a decided turn for the better. My voice didn't fade and sound weak and tired until late afternoon." Then, she added assurance that she is up to the task of having guests:

140

Really Esther, I'll go ahead with my regular work and we'll make things very simple. As for housecleaning, I've been "picking" at it for weeks, and what doesn't get done can go hang. I went through all the accumulations of years and gave away six cartons of junk to the Salvation Army; went through all closets and cupboards, but honestly, they need it again. I varnished the woodwork, washed the draperies, and now the sun porch is sanded and we'll varnish it tomorrow. So make your plans, and I'll lay low and get well before you come. I'm really feeling fine, working just as I always did, and maybe a little bit more. It is just my croaky voice. It was never very strong in the first place, and very apt to go funny when I had colds, remember?

This last line gives me a jolt of recognition, for I too am apt to lose my voice when I get a cold. Also, my grandmother's zeal for getting rid of clutter and her satisfaction in deep cleaning feels like a soul connection. How I love going through closets, drawers, even the dreaded basement, and pitching everything that is not useful or beautiful! And almost nothing feels better than the feeling of freshly washed and pressed curtains, steam-cleaned carpets, or a fresh coat of paint on the walls.

Ruth's next letter, May 6, is filled with excitement over the impending visit.

I can't tell you how glad I am that you are coming! Something just sings inside of me when I think of having you and Freddie [Esther's youngest son] here. I told Frank you offered to paint the bathroom and he said, "She can do any darn thing she wants to. I only know it'll be good for you to have her here." He has already made plans to take you to the Flame (Duluth night club) which is his idea of tops in entertainment.

Exactly one month later, after a wonderful and lengthy visit from her sister and little nephew, a bereft Ruth sits down again at the typewriter:

It seems impossible that you aren't somewhere around, or at least in Duluth, and coming over soon! I've never been as lonesome as I was yesterday after you and Freddie had left. Tried to work off my blues and—you guessed it!—worked too hard.

Part of that work was in anticipation of another house-guest, her mother-in-law, "Mutti," who would stay with the family for some time.

My grandmother's next letter, dated June 16, includes a few lines that are a harbinger of things to come:

We've had a few chilly-bright days, and they are hard on my neuritis. Yesterday I had to take the stairs one foot at a time, as my right leg ached like a toothache. Today it is the whole back, and I can't sit, stand or lie down, in comfort.

Then, as if to reassure her sister: "My throat feels fine, and as I said, my voice is good. I don't mind a little rheumatism then."

But in a letter dated July 8, any pretense of recovery is over. Though she was still concealing the truth from her children, she confided in Esther, describing the pain that she was feeling off and on throughout her body.

Her next letter, written on July 26, is equally frank, though she is anticipating with pleasure another visit from Esther:

This can't be long. My left shoulder is one big toothache, and it extends to my back when I sit here and type. I could take a pill, but want to be able to take one in an hour when I go to bed. I'm really beginning to understand dope fiends now: as it is a fight not to just go to bed early so I can take a pill and relax.

THE REST OF MY grandmother's letters are handwritten in pencil, from her bed at St. Joseph's hospital. Saturday, September 5, she writes:

This arrangement, though expensive, is surely wonderful for us all. I get the best of care, and quiet. Mutti runs things at home with Marian's help, washing, ironing and scrubbing. I know they are well-fed and looked after, which is Heaven to me. Frank gets lonely. Is here twice a day and also drops in after hours at night when he gets a good quit [quitting time]. He just walks in, gives me ice water and we visit until he feels like going. No attention to the rules.

Tuesday, September 12, Ruth is "dopey" from medication, but writes to acknowledge a box of homemade candy Esther has sent in the mail. The sweet account of hearing from each child about his or her first day at school and then surprising them with Aunt Esther's homemade candy fills me with admiration for my grandmother. It must have been very difficult for her to languish in a sterile hospital room, fuzzy with medication to relieve the constant pain, barely able to talk; yet the pleasure of this time with her children is obvious. She would write in one of her last letters to my father, "I love you every minute, and my family is right here in my heart all the time." I truly believe that her every thought from the hospital bed was about her family's well-being.

However, words written in her last letter to Esther leave me shaking my head.

Thank goodness school takes their attention now and Nature rather takes care of Trouble for them. Youngsters just naturally don't go around worrying, but finally accept situations and are happy again.

Perhaps my grandmother believed this to be true of her children, or maybe it is just what she wanted to believe. The pretense she had maintained for their sake for so long might have created a separate reality that enabled her to write these words from her deathbed. I wonder, though, if she was genuinely unaware of the emotional and spiritual devastation that would follow in the wake of her passing.

MY GRANDMOTHER'S GRAVE is bathed by the sun as I mull over this drama, played out over half a century ago. I am tired, JoJo is getting restless, and my visit here is almost over. But there are so many questions I wish I could ask her and things I would like her to know. Why did you die this way? Not why cancer—anyone can get cancer—but why the long charade, the shutting down of honest fears and regrets? Why did no one visit your grave? Was it your Victorian sense of correctness that kept you from confiding more of the pain you were feeling, the pain you must have felt over losing everything you held dear—your children, husband, your cherished sisters and mother, your life?

Do you know that, fifty years after your death, my father's voice becomes small and pinched when speaking of you, and Aunt Marian still cries over the last letter you wrote to her?

I wonder if it would have been different if Ruth's children could have talked openly with her during her dying time, if she had looked them in the eyes and acknowledged this dreadful thing that was happening, but affirming that one day it would not feel so dreadful. Would it have been different if she had told them that death and loss and grieving are a natural part of our celebrated lives, and we all walk through these times but never alone? Would it have been different if she had held my father's hand and assured him that God would comfort and guide him all of his days, as surely as he was holding her in his mighty arms, preparing to take her spirit home?

I wonder if her legacy would have been less painful had my father and his sisters been able to grieve, if they had taken many trips instead of none back to this place, where I now sit, to lay down flowers and weep. Then would the pain of their mother's passing have ebbed into a sweet ache of remembrance, instead of remaining a heavy blanket of sadness?

I will never know the answer to these questions, but I do know this: My grandmother's story has moved me. Her sad death has had a mysterious resilience, so that its effect has been able to jump across generations and lodge in my heart. Reading her letters, thumbing through Great-Aunt Vi's diary, standing at my grandmother's grave—the pathos of her life has touched me. We have never met, yet I've inherited some of her gifts and carry them on—her ability to write, her heart for teaching, and her love of music and the outdoors. In the end, her name and very self are things of which I am proud.

My grandmother's short life has left an indelible imprint on my earthly journey, a reminder of the mysterious human connectedness we all share. Her story has inspired me to feel and express every emotion along life's path. Her painful leaving makes a poignant case for the magnificent release of grieving. Her grave reminds me to seek beauty in the heartrending process of living but not to miss any part of it, especially the exquisite agony of the dying time.

Ultimately I will live my own life and die my own death, but my grandmother travels with me. I am not alone.

seven

Crossroads

Unexpected Meetings

But the effect of her being on those around her was incalculably diffusive: for the growing good of the world is partly dependent on unhistoric acts; and that things are not so ill with you and me as they might have been, is half owing to the number who lived faithfully a hidden life, and rest in unvisited tombs.

GEORGE ELIOT, MIDDLEMARCH

ONE OF THE DELICIOUS mysteries of life is the way we find others and they find us. Though millions of people inhabit the earth, two imperfect paths will cross at a perfect moment along seemingly disparate journeys. I've come to believe that these chance meetings, which enrich life beyond measure, are not accidental. They remind me how all of life is connected and how, in those moments of feeling disconnected, we must reach out and embrace what grounds us.

IT'S 824 MILES from my driveway in Nashville to my mother's hometown of Menomonie, Wisconsin—a thirteen-and-a-half-hour drive with good road conditions, a grueling undertaking if made in one day. I remember as a girl making the much shorter drive north from Decatur, squeezed into the back of our family's Volkswagen Beetle, on our way to visit my mom's parents, Grandma and Grandpa Huber. After thirty years of working a farm out on East Townline Road, my grandparents had settled into a quaint, two-story house in town, near Stout University.

I have vivid memories of that house and its patina of wonderful oldness. I can still smell its sweet, musty fragrance when I bury my face in the linens and embroidered pillowcases I inherited from Grandma Huber.

My grandparents are gone now, and when I drive to Menomonie, I head for the opposite side of town, a unique landmark of this sleepy college community called the Bolo Inn.

I first stayed at the Bolo while on the 1997 trip I made to Wisconsin with my parents. We rambled down the memory lane of their respective childhood towns, a trip that culminated in the frustrating, not-quite-finding of my grandmother Ruth's grave.

The inn, which sits at the edge of town, is a Menomonie treasure, owned and operated by members of the same family for almost fifty years. It was named for the founding owner's beloved black Labrador retriever and has the charm of an old motor inn found along Route 66 in its heyday. The sprawling establishment included three rows of quaint rooms, each charmingly decorated in Laura Ashley country style and opening onto a parking area. The motel was surrounded by a lovely oasis of tall trees, a small forest in the midst of an otherwise industrialized part of town.

Walking into the restaurant/lounge to register for our stay was like stepping back into the 1960s. My eyes had to adjust from the bright outdoors to fully appreciate the denlike coziness of this dusky, windowless space. Mirrors hung on the paneled walls, black and red Naugahyde-covered chairs were at each table, tiny white Christmas lights lined the edge of the ceiling, and heavy red velvet drapes hung from ceiling to floor.

The decor was almost entirely devoted to the memory of Bolo. The specially designed, wall-to-wall carpet was imprinted with silhouettes of the Labrador retriever's head, hanging lamps around the bar glowed through similar silhouette cut-outs, and a life-size oil painting of Bolo hung from the wall of the main dining room. The black hunting dog's image also adorned the napkins, place mats, and menus. As a dog lover, I thought this shrine to the majestic Bolo completely appropriate and wonderful.

Up the road from the Bolo, heading north on Highway 25, was my other compelling destination—my great-grandparents' farm, nestled against the hills of Sherman Township. Though the farm has been out of our family now for over half a century, I've come to think of this place as the Old Huber Farm. It has been speculated that the house, built in 1910 by my great-grandfather, who immigrated to America from Switzerland in 1867, had been ordered from a Sears catalog. It is made almost completely from formed concrete stone.

An old family picture, taken shortly after the house was built, shows my great-grandparents, Henry and Ernestine, standing on the front steps, with their four grown sons sitting on the stone railing or leaning against the Victorian-style pillars that support the front porch. The house rises proudly against the wooded hills behind it, and you can see in this picture my great-grandfather's passion: rows and rows of carefully cultivated grapevines winding up the slope to the right of the house. He chose the home site on this land, I'd heard, because it reminded him of where he'd grown up in Switzerland. Today the view from the road in front of the house is still much the same as it was back when my great-grandparents lived here.

My grandfather, Fred Huber, brought my grandmother, Lulu Jabusch Huber, here to live with his parents for a short time after they married in 1913, before moving out to the farm on East Townline Road. But Grandma Huber didn't get along well with her in-laws, especially Great-Grandmother Ernestine. Though I can only guess at the whole story, their relationship apparently was fractious enough to poison relations between the families for years to come.

Ironically I would come to spend more time inside the house on the Old Huber Farm than my own mother had.

DRIVING BY MY GREAT-GRANDPARENTS' farm in 1997 planted a seed of interest in my writer's heart, a legacy I felt compelled to explore. I remember thinking at first sight: *There are few places in the world that remain so unchanged.* We had driven up to the house but didn't go inside since the current owner had no family connection to us whatsoever. Yet the stately presence of that great stone house—in picture and now in memory—haunted me.

Two years later, on the same trip that led me to find my grandmother Ruth's grave, I went back to Menomonie, hoping to learn more about my great-grandparents' farm. I was pleasantly surprised to discover I'm distantly related to just about everyone who lives in this cross section of farmland. One of these relatives, a dear woman named Lenora—the widow of one of my mother's cousins—knows something about almost everyone in the farmlands around Menomonie. So, on my behalf, she called up Arnold Geissler, the man who had owned and lived on my great-grandparents' farm for fifty years.

"The great-granddaughter of Henry Huber would like to meet you," she said. "She's from Nashville, Tennessee, and plays the violin and writes books. She wants to talk with you about the farm."

Arnold Geissler agreed to my visit.

The winding road that dips into the Old Huber Farm soon disappears up a long wooded hill. On that hot June day in 1999, I drove along that dusty road with an efficient agenda. Armed with a yellow lined notepad and a camera, I hoped to grill Mr. Geissler for details on the farm and my great-grandparents and take pictures of the inside of the house. Frankly, I was much more interested in absorbing the atmosphere of the place than getting to know Arnold Geissler, though I was grateful he'd agreed to the visit.

I pulled into the driveway and parked near the side entrance to the house, where he'd already pushed open the screen door to welcome me. He led me through the kitchen, into the dining room, where I was immediately enchanted by the built-in china cabinet, dating from 1910, and silver-painted radiators hugging the walls. Within minutes, I knew I'd stumbled onto hidden treasure.

Arnie Geissler turned out to be one of those people you feel you've known a long time. He was eighty-three at the time, retired from farming for just three years, and recently widowed. His wife of fifty-three years, Lucille, with whom he'd worked side by side on the farm, had passed away at Easter.

We talked, the conversation drifting from the farm to the escapades of Arnie's youth, his wartime service for which he'd been decorated with a Purple Heart and three Bronze Stars, then again to the recent loss of his wife. I felt the focus of my visit shift from my great-grandparents' story to a fascination with his. The enchanting Arnie Geissler turned out to be one of the lovely surprises of my life.

On that day a wonderful friendship began that would span three years—the rest of Arnie's life. Every time I made my way north, I'd drop in to see Arnie, and each time he visited his great-grandchildren in Dickson, Tennessee, just an hour south of my home in Nashville, I'd meet him there for an hour or two. In between visits we'd exchange an occasional phone call. Our conversations always ended on the same note, one of gratitude that the paths of our lives had intersected, despite amazing odds. We shared a mutual enjoyment for what we'd discovered in each other's soul.

From the very beginning, Arnie impressed me as a person with a story to tell. As anyone who knew Arnie Geissler would say, he loved to recall his life story and told it often. I heard the same story every time I visited him, but I never tired of hearing it because it was so interesting. The more I heard it, the more I felt it was a story we would all do well to hear.

Arnie was of the second generation of American Geisslers. He was born in 1915, one of what would be eight children, in a generation that would witness two world wars and the Great Depression. His grandparents had come over from Austria, and for the first five years of his life, he spoke German better than he did English.

You could say Arnie was a true twentieth-century man, for his life spanned nearly all of it. He was one of what are now a dwindling number who could testify to a time in history almost impossible to imagine, a time we'll never see again. He grew up in an era devoid of entitlement, believing that life was something you carved out for yourself with the sweat of your brow and the strength of your convictions, believing that in America anything was possible if you worked and prayed hard enough.

When Arnie was in seventh grade, just twelve years old, he dropped out of school to shoulder the responsibility of running the family farm. His father had been disabled in an accident, and Arnie, the oldest son still living at home, just stepped up to a responsibility he felt was his. This same sense of responsibility led him, on the day after his twenty-fifth birthday, in December 1941, to enlist in the armed services, two days after the Japanese attacked Pearl Harbor. He said good-bye to his red-haired girlfriend, Lucille, promising to marry her if he made it back from the war.

He was only one of the thousands of anonymous war heroes whose willingness to serve their country provided me with a life of freedom and opportunity that I often take for granted. Most of the men who survived World War II came home to live faithful but unheralded lives and eventually rested in unvisited graves.

Hearing Arnie talk about what it was like to survive the campaign of Merrill's Marauders in the Burma theater, one of just 357 of a group of men originally numbering 2,800, brought not just his sacrifice but the sacrifice made by all who have served in the military into terribly clear focus. He chopped through jungles of bamboo with a machete, ate unspeakably bad food, watched men all around him sicken and die from malaria, dysentery, and typhoid, and somehow got up each day and continued to do the impossible.

He told me that he never thought about dying, but believed that his mother, who prayed the rosary for him every day, had literally prayed him safely home from the war.

Each time Arnie got to the end of this story, his eyes would water and he'd shake his head from side to side and mutter, "It couldn't have been me, it must have been somebody else." I suppose that in order to live with the horrors he had seen, the sounds he had heard, and the terrible smell of death, he had to compartmentalize the long, surreal nightmare as a memory of another person from another lifetime.

156

The forty months he spent fighting during World War II surely left indelible emotional and spiritual scars that he carried with him his whole life. Yet I never detected a shred of self-pity or expectation of praise. Perhaps the qualities I admired most in him were his joy of giving to others and the absence of any sense of entitlement. His whole life seemed to be one of matter-of-fact service—in all that he gave to his childhood family, his own wife and children, his country, and his beloved farm—he genuinely expected nothing in return.

When I stumbled into Arnie's world, it was on the whim of visiting an old house that had captured my imagination. It would seem that we had nothing in common: I was forty-one. He was eighty-three. I lived in Tennessee. He lived in Wisconsin. I was a musician, wellness trainer, and writer. He'd spent his whole life working a farm.

Still, we found so much shared interest. I was enchanted with the Old Huber Farm. Arnie considered it his "little piece of heaven on earth." He loved to rest in a lawn chair right outside the door on the side porch, where what he called the perfect breeze came through. He'd sit there for hours in good weather, with his dog, Tippy, a scruffy retriever mix who, with adoration, stayed close to the chair for hours, one little paw in Arnie's hand.

When we talked on the phone, I'd always ask with—I confess—a bit of envy, "What's it like up there?"

"Oh," Arnie would say, "it's the most beautiful place in the world."

SOMETIMES I WONDER why Arnie's stories, the Old Huber Farm, and stories about my mother's childhood there have so fascinated me. I can explain my fervent interest in the past, with all things old and authentic, only as part of my quest to feel at home inside myself. I grew up in the Baby Boom generation, privileged, well-educated, not lacking any creature comfort. I have experienced, in many ways, an environment like that of a hothouse flower. I honed my musical and creative gifts in conservatory practice rooms and chased after crazy career dreams, thinking of no one but myself. But these things were all external—hopes and goals and lists of things to accomplish that I thought would make me look better on the outside.

They never did make me feel any different, any more perfect—that grail I had ruthlessly pursued—on the inside.

It's no coincidence, then, that I was drawn back to the solid, gritty lives of my ancestors. Although I too have worked hard in my career pursuits, my efforts pale in comparison to the work of their hands. My mother's parents led a grueling life, working a dairy farm through the Depression era, without the comfort of any modern convenience. My poor dying grandmother, Ruth, struggled to live for five years after her disfiguring surgery, trying to hide from her family her illness and suffering.

Their enduring legacies humble me. The tawdriness of our times and the self-absorption of our culture make me ache for the solid ground my grandparents stood on, ground that Arnie

Geissler fought to defend. I watch the spectacle of popular culture, and even the drama of my own life, and feel regret.

Yet, maybe, if I look deeply and honestly, I can find something else there too.

ONE COLD NIGHT in February 2002, I stood in front of Arnie Geissler's farmhouse, the house that my great-grandparents had built nearly a century ago. The house was dark and empty.

I'd ridden by the house earlier that day, behind the hearse carrying Arnie's body, a funeral procession passing one last time through the farm he loved so dearly to his final resting place, several miles up Highway 25. The sight of his dog, Tippy, standing in front of the porch, wagging his tail, excited by all the commotion on that seldom traveled road, brought a great lump to my throat. I could not help but think of all the hours Arnie and Tippy had sat there, enjoying the breeze and the view, which remains beautifully unblemished by the passage of time.

On one of my last visits to the farm before Arnie passed away, I asked him how, after all the pain he'd endured in his life—which included fighting a world war and outliving a son, a grandson, and his beloved Lucille—he had kept a joyful view of life. He looked at me kind of funny and just said, "I don't know any better." When I pressed him to be more specific, he simply said, "I've been very lucky that in all the places I've been and all that's happened to me, I've had a good life."

A good life was lived here, I thought, standing in the dark in front of the farmhouse. I'd stopped here on a whim, much as I did the first time I met Arnie, to say a final good-bye to a friend I'd sorely miss. The sight of the house without him in it chilled me—so empty, so much lost.

But the stars shone amazingly close and bright that night. I looked around at the valley that encircled Arnie's little piece of heaven. How little had changed since my great-grandparents established this farm in 1910. How much everything changes now. *Yes*, I thought, *everything changes—and I don't want it to . . .*

My grandparents' house in Menomonie where I played as a child is gone, bulldozed to provide parking space for Stout University. The Bolo Inn has been sold and will likely be torn down to accommodate a mega-sized supermarket, just another ugly, undistinguished building to scar the landscape on the edge of town.

I looked around at the farm, ethereally beautiful in the growing darkness, and silently mourned. Will this change too? Will the legacy of this land, the work of my great-grandparents and Arnie Geissler evaporate in time, beyond all memory?

The words of Isaiah 40:8 flashed through my mind: "The grass withers, the flower fades, but the word of our God stands forever." I think of Arnie's steadfast faith in the Lord, how often he'd said to me, "I'm a great believer in prayer."

I closed my eyes and prayed, "Lord, please let this mean something. Please let this earthly journey not be for nothing."

When I looked up at the sky, the stars seemed brighter somehow. I could hear Arnie's words from the front porch: "A little piece of heaven." A verse from the Book of Matthew came to me: "Well done, good and faithful servant; you were faithful over a few things, I will make you ruler over many things. Enter into the joy of your lord" (Matt. 25:21).

I took one last fond look at the house and got back into my car, shifted into drive, and headed toward town for my last night's stay at the Bolo Inn. I was plowing into a night I did not know. How easy it is, I thought, to stumble in the dark or take a wrong turn, so easy to lose one's way. Yet, instinctively, my hand on the wheel, like my heart, was finding the way.

eight

Yieldings

Breathing Freely

Maybe a lot of people could say the same—I think they could; the squeak between living and not living is pretty tight—but I have had a lucky life. That is to say that I know I've been lucky. Beyond that, the question is if I have not been also blessed, as I believe I have—and, beyond that, even called.

WENDELL BERRY, JAYBER CROW

IN MY THIRTIES I began a long journey back to my essential self, a journey through time and geography to connect with a little girl who knew the gift of breathing freely. What started as a quest for right living turned into something much more profound. At the center of my life were little red flags that indicated something wasn't working. There were struggles with various compulsions, an inability to stay in relationships, a debilitating absence of joy. As I confronted the definitive milestones along the ruptured landscape of my personal life, I learned this seldom spoken truth: No matter how often you revisit old injuries, you never get rid of the pain, but by breathing into that pain, much like a woman in labor, you can claim some peace in coexistence with it. You can diminish its ability to extinguish your God-given resilience of spirit, the light that shines from within. Spirit and light, from the beginning of time, have always led human beings in the direction of joy.

In fact pain, instead of searing us into cynicism or collapsing us into ourselves, can be a freeing baptism by fire. In embracing every age we've been—the naïveté of our youth or failings of our older selves—we continue our journey in flawed wholeness. The pain dulls in time but is always with us, like a piece of luggage we carry, reminding us of lessons learned, wisdom gained, and the importance of compassion.

I've found that being present with the horrible is the price exacted by the beautiful, part of the eternal landscape of our existence, the age-old struggle between good and evil, darkness and light, despair and hope. Against the ugly backdrop of my sexual wounding is the beautiful respect that my husband extends to me, as I wade through layers of understandable resistance to meet him in our intimate life together. Allowing the entirety of my being to travel with me has colored this snapshot of my journey with joy.

In the midst of these travels, I found my way back to faith, after abandoning it for twenty years. I've often described my faith as a lurching spiritual journey, and so it continues today. After the initial euphoria of my midlife conversion, I found plenty of ways to add my relationship with Jesus to the list of things I figured I'd never do well enough. The aura of Stepford-wife sterility that permeates some Christian arenas has driven me back into the corner of my lurking agnosticism more than once. But ultimately I cannot escape this truth: Only in knowing that a sovereign God continues to help me live and write my story will I enjoy that coveted prize—the gift of breathing freely.

There's much richness in my flawed and flailing spiritual tapestry—like the lines of Scripture that I memorize in fits and starts, less for theological depth than the instant relief they provide in a moment of need. I grab onto them as a lifeline, when the unreasonable fear and perfectionism that continue to dog me threaten to pull me into dark valleys. *I will lift up my eyes to the hills*, says the psalmist, reminding me, *from whence comes my help? My help comes from the* LORD, *who made heaven and earth* (Ps. 121:1–2). I can loosen my grip on the armrest of the airplane seat, and the stranglehold of my expectations, when I utter these words that remind me in whose plan I truly find rest.

This unsteady walk has revealed to me also a holy participation throughout my life, even, if not especially, during those desert years. In the twists and turns of my wayward path, there were oasis people who showed up to give me direction: Sherry, toward musical freedom and Nashville; John Hartford, toward creative integrity; my husband John, who, after my string of abusive relationships, has provided the safest human harbor I've known.

This holy participation has continued in the sweetness of my first grown-up church home, Covenant Presbyterian, in Nashville. There, in the familiar order of worship, the formal, traditional service, and the hymns I sang as a child, I have found the firmness of ground that I'd yearned for but missed often in my journey. As I sit through the sermons, struggling to keep my mind from wandering, I am always rewarded by a sentence or a phrase that sends me scrambling for a pew pencil, to commit it to paper and then to memory. "Our entire life is lived before the face of God," the preacher says. *Eeeek,* I think to myself, *my entire life is lived before the face of God?* But then from the pulpit come words of encouragement just when I need them. "Keep doing what is beautiful. The harvest takes time."

Perhaps most profoundly convincing of this holy participation, and hardest for me to describe, is the real, ongoing sensation I experience today as I set violin bow to violin strings. After years of struggling with music as a form of punishment, identity, and ego gratification, I have surrendered this outlet of my creativity to the workings of divine grace. It has become over time my freest and most profound means of conversation with God.

Then there is the freedom of feeling at home in my life. I have learned to be grateful for my fulfilling, if less than sensational, career and grateful for the gift of our small house, complete with torn linoleum on the kitchen floor, thanks to the teething escapades of our newest puppy, Misty-Lou. I have come to expect daily surprises of grace that lift me up out of the discontent of my thwarted desires, like watching in thrilled amazement through the back windows of our house as the beautiful sunset writes dramatic patterns and colors against the darkening sky. I measure my life so much less by appearance, acquisitions, and achievements and more by the standard of my friend Arnie, who at eighty-six, looking back at the measure of his life, felt he'd been lucky.

Today my knees make little creaking sounds despite my years of athletic training, and I can no longer deny the fact that when I look in the mirror, at forty-four, my skin is slowly getting too big for my body. But no amount of vanity will ever convince me to erase what I see there, for along with the crow's feet is a calm clarity in my eyes that didn't exist ten years ago. Perched somewhere in the middle of life, I am able to give thanks to God in the very best way I know how for this gift of life, by saying what ten years ago I could not say. I love my life. In all its pain and imperfection, I am grateful for this journey.

The journey never ends—my life stretches before me, like the foggy image of a Polaroid snapshot, slowly developing.

Acknowledgments

I AM GRATEFUL to the many people who have encouraged me in the writing of this book. Thanks to everyone at Baker Book House, especially Jeanette Thomason and Mary L. Suggs for their editorial guidance. Thanks to Susan Browne and Cheryl Van Andel for the beautiful cover design and to Jim Shea for the lovely back cover photo.

I continue to be blessed with friends and colleagues who make enormous personal and professional contributions to my creative career. Heartfelt thanks to Chris Davis, Gary Glover, David Dunham, Jim Dausch, Susan Crumpton, Kathy Chiavola, Karen Miller, Amy Grant, Sherry Downie, Lisa Bamford, and Ian Sears.

Finally, I am deeply grateful for my family, both immediate and extended, and for the love and support of my husband, John Burrell.

Ruth McGinnis is an author, recording artist, and wellness professional who uses creative diversity to celebrate life and encourage others to do the same. She is the author of *Living the Good Life*, a guide to overall well-being, based on her many years' experience as a certified personal trainer.

A graduate of the Juilliard School of Music (B.M., M.M.), Ruth is a violinist/fiddler who has performed and recorded with Amy Grant, Michael W. Smith, Vince Gill, and the late John Hartford. Her instrumental recordings, *Songs for the Good Life* (2000), and *Breathing Freely* (2002), feature Celtic, sacred, and classical melodies, and her trademark, classical-crossover style.

Ruth lives in Nashville, Tennessee, with her husband, John Burrell, four dogs, and one cat.

For more information about Ruth's books and CDs, visit her web site at:

www.ruthmcginnis.com